WHERE TRUTH LIES

WHERE TRUTH LIES

A GUIDE TO UNDERSTANDING WHAT PEOPLE *REALLY* ARE SAYING

By Stanley B. Burke

WHERE TRUTH LIES. Copyright © 2024 by Stanley B. Burke. All rights reserved. Printed in the United States of America. Precision Intelligence Consulting, LLC
www.precisionintelligenceconsulting.com

Editing, layout, cover design: Mary Coffman-Burke, www.write-space.com
Cover photo: gremlin @ istockphoto.com

ISBN 979-8-218-40802-2

A percentage of gross proceeds from this book will be donated to Empower House
P.O. Box 1007, Fredericksburg, VA 22402
www.empowerhouseva.org

IMPORTANT: Reading this book and completing its exercises does not, by itself, qualify you to be an expert in analyzing what people communicate. The information provided in this book is the result of knowledge drawn from the author's years of personal experience, education, interviews, specialized training, and research. This book is not a substitute for a thorough, well-planned investigation and should not be considered all-inclusive.

The author wrote it with the information available at the time of its publication and the author assumes that the information contained in it is accurate. Should additional information or materials become available at a later date this book may be revised or changed. The methodologies explained in this book are considered investigative tools that may assist or support inquiry into a statement. The methodologies contained in this book do not conclusively predict if a statement contains veracity or deception and is not testimonial in nature. This book is not legal advice or legal service for the reader and is not intended to act as a substitute for legal advice or legal service. The information contained in this book is not a replacement for any laws in effect in the reader's jurisdiction.

To Mary.
Your vision and never-ending encouragement are what made this book possible.

CONTENTS

Introduction 1

Chapter 1: Hiding Guilty Information 5

Chapter 2: Occurrence of Significance 9

Chapter 3: High-Quality Sensory Details 27

Chapter 4: High-Quality Locational Details 39

Comprehensive Exercise 1 47

Chapter 5: Pivot Words 51

Comprehensive Exercise 2 63

Chapter 6: Irrelevant Information 67

Comprehensive Exercise 3 85

Chapter 7: Time Markers 91

Comprehensive Exercise 4 101

Chapter 8: Statement Gaps 107

Comprehensive Exercise 5 115

Chapter 9: Gap Cover Words 119

Comprehensive Exercise 6 125

Chapter 10: Uncompleted-Action Words 131

Comprehensive Exercise 7 137

Chapter 11: Non-Specific Transit Words 143

Final Comprehensive Exercise 149

Summary Chart 161

References 165

Notes 170

INTRODUCTION

Have you ever talked to a salesperson, read a newspaper article, heard a politician, or listened to a podcast and then asked yourself, "What was that person really saying?" If so, you've picked up the right book. I wrote *Where Truth Lies: A Guide to Understanding What People Really Are Saying* to compile what I learned in my more than 35 years of experience as an FBI Special Agent and as a law-enforcement educator. In that time I have analyzed hundreds of statements from victims, witnesses, suspects, and other law-enforcement officers–including conversations, interviews, interrogations, speeches, press conferences, and sales pitches–to try to pinpoint a person's intent in the words they choose. Are they being truthful? Are they trying to hide their own or someone else's guilt?

In 2014, a police detective from Montgomery County, Maryland, asked me to assist him with a cold-case investigation involving two young sisters, Sheila and Katherine Lyon, who had disappeared from a Maryland shopping center in 1975. He said that a team of detectives from his agency had interviewed a person of interest and that they had asked him to write a statement about his life. The detective asked me to examine that six-page statement to see if it contained any information indicating that the person of interest had participated in the disappearance of the girls.

My examination of the man's statement showed that he may have been harboring

A 1975 Cold Case
The Lyon Sisters

Lewiston Morning Journal, 24 August 1975.

guilty knowledge. I gave the detective suggested questions for re-interviewing the man; questions designed specifically to explore the areas of the letter where I believed the author could be hiding guilty knowledge. Several weeks later the detective told me his team had re-interviewed the person of interest and that he had admitted to taking the girls from the shopping center back in 1975. He later was convicted of murdering the two girls.

What exactly did I do to help? I simply looked at every word in his statement and examined the purpose of each one. In doing so I found some word usage that I questioned. That's it! In everyday life, you may do the same thing when you listen to what someone says or read something that someone writes. However, you probably don't refer to your impressions as results. More likely you call them gut feelings. This book will introduce you to methodologies that will help you organize those gut feelings into science- and research-based results.

ABOUT THIS BOOK

I wrote this book as a supplement to my course called Investigative Statement Analysis, but it can be useful to anyone interested in understanding how to look for truth and for hidden lies in what people say.

Chapter 1 explains why and how people manipulate language. Chapters 2 through 11 explain the various methodologies that I use to examine individual statements. I provide sample statements to illustrate each methodology, practice exercises with analysis to understand that methodology, and tips for using the methodology.

Along the way I have included comprehensive exercises. This is the time to get out your pencil and work through the exercises! As you do so, don't worry if your answers don't exactly match mine. What's important is that you understand the essence of the concepts. The final exercise puts it all together.

The information in this book comes from anecdotal research, empirical research, textbooks, videos, periodicals, and professional journals representing the areas of psychology, communication, and linguistics.

The statements used in this book are fictionalized statements based on or inspired by statements that I personally encountered during my career.

Throughout this book I use the word "author" or the phrase "author's statement" to refer to a person giving a statement in a conversation, in an interrogation, on a phone call, or even through a text message or email.

WHAT IS *NOT* THE INTENT OF THIS BOOK

It is NOT the intent of this book to give you the ability to determine with absolute certainty if someone is lying or not. There are no language analysis techniques or methods of which I am aware that will allow you to do that. If you know of such a technique or method please let me know.

WHAT *IS* THE INTENT OF THIS BOOK

It IS the intent of this book to introduce you to specific methodologies for examining statements—some of the same methodologies I use when I examine a statement. It is also the intent of this book to make you more curious about statements and encourage you to ask questions about them. Enjoy!

CHAPTER 1: HIDING GUILTY INFORMATION

Humans developed language around 150,000 to 200,000 years ago (Pagel, 2017) to communicate information about food and water sources, shelters, and threats. Over time, we began to use language to express feelings, thoughts, ideas, wants, and desires. Perhaps inevitably, we then learned to manipulate language to protect ourselves from situations that might expose us to punishment, embarrassment, or shame.

To illustrate, let's go back in time to a small village where a farmer named Johan has stolen some gold nuggets from the local cobbler. The moment Johan stole those gold nuggets he became the not-so-lucky owner of guilty or culpable knowledge. Having knowledge of the theft and knowing that the exposure of this knowledge surely would cause him punishment, embarrassment, or shame, Johan likely would try to hide that guilty knowledge.

The village's chief law enforcement official, Sheriff Clue, conducts an investigation into the missing gold and suspects Johan of the theft. When she confronts Johan and asks him if he stole the gold, it's unlikely his response would be, "I took it!" His answer more likely would be something similar to one of these:

"I didn't know the cobbler had any gold."
"Why would I take the cobbler's gold?"
"I'm the last person that would steal the cobbler's gold."
"Maybe the cobbler misplaced the gold."

Why would these responses be expected? Because as a

> *"Man is not what he thinks he is; he is what he hides."*
>
> – Andre Malraux

member of a species that has been defending itself against threats for thousands of years, Johan naturally recognizes the sheriff as a threat to exposing his guilt and he reacts accordingly. This is a classic fight or flight response. In choosing to respond in any of those ways, Johan picks fleeing from the sheriff's inquiry through the words he uses rather than fighting back with his fists or a weapon.

How did Johan use his words to flee from the sheriff? By using Irrelevant Information (Chapter 6) to avoid the sheriff's inquiry and to minimize the chance of revealing his guilty information. Johan's desire likely was for the sheriff to accept an answer that would not cause Johan punishment, embarrassment, or shame–and to stop the sheriff's questioning of him. Interestingly, Johan never says he didn't steal the gold.

In the remainder of this book I will examine written and oral responses that people use to avoid exposing guilty knowledge. Each chapter focuses on one of 10 language-analysis methods. When properly applied these methods will give you insight into a subject's choice of words and a better understanding of what the subject said and why they said it.

TIPS

TIP 1   **LANGUAGE STRATEGIES MAY BE USED TO HIDE GUILTY INFORMATION**

When confronted with questions that may expose guilty knowledge, some people may use language strategies to avoid revealing that knowledge. But other people hiding guilty knowledge may choose to avoid stress and simply tell the truth.

TIP 2   **MAKE SURE THE QUESTION IS ANSWERED**

Think back to Johan's possible responses to the sheriff's question, "Did you take the cobbler's gold?" What should have been the sheriff's next step if Johan had given one of those responses? The sheriff should recognize that Johan did not answer her question and should attempt to get an answer. For instance, the response *"I would never take the cobbler's gold!"* does not answer the question. The sheriff should see that she didn't ask if he *would have* stolen the gold, but if he *did* steal the gold.

TIP 3   **CONSIDER HABITUAL LANGUAGE**

Sometimes people use words that may indicate they are avoiding exposing guilty knowledge, when they aren't doing that. This could happen when an author uses habitual language–words used repeatedly out of conversational habit and not intended for deception.

An example of this is the word *like*. This is a Pivot Word (Chapter 5) that could be used to avoid exposing guilty knowledge OR it could be part of someone's habitual language.

To illustrate: If the sheriff asks Johan to tell her about his day and Johan says, "Me and my friends walked to the square and visited some merchants. We then went to the stables to feed the horses and muck some stalls. After that we went to a pub and ate. When we were finished, I like went home." What does *like* mean in his statement? Did he go home or not? Johan could be using *like* as a strategy to avoid commitment about going home. Did he slip by the cobbler's store and steal the gold?

Now suppose *like* is part of Johan's habitual language or language baseline, and he gives this response: "We like walked to the square and like we visited some merchants. We then like went to the stables to feed horses and muck some stalls. After that we like went to a pub and ate. When we were finished, I like went home." In this example Johan uses the word *like* habitually. It appears to be part of his language baseline. In this case Sheriff Clue would dismiss the possibility that Johan is using the word *like* to avoid exposing guilty knowledge.

CHAPTER 2: OCCURRENCE OF SIGNIFICANCE

This chapter examines the Occurrence of Significance and answers these questions:
• What is an Occurrence of Significance?
• How do we recognize a statement's Occurrence of Significance?
• What does an Occurrence of Significance tell us about an author's commitment to their statement?

When humans first began communicating we did so primarily to share important information such as the location of food and water sources, shelter, or potential threats. Although current-day communications are not as likely to provide information about food sources or shelter locations, we still share experiences when we have been involved in a significant incident, problem, issue, or concern—what I call Occurrences of Significance.

Imagine a coworker comes up to you and says without being prompted, "I just had a drink of water from the fountain," and then walks away. You would probably consider that an odd thing to say because your coworker didn't express anything of significance. Most people do not go out of their way to tell you they had a drink of water unless something of significance occurred during that process. They had a drink of water, so what?

But if your coworker says, "I just had a drink of water from the fountain and it tasted salty," that statement would probably mean something to you because it contains an Occurrence of

> *"Happiness is when what you think, what you say, and what you do are in harmony."*
>
> *– Mahatma Gandhi*

Significance, specifically that the water tasted salty.

What does all of this have to do with understanding what a person says? Simply this: When most people experience a notable problem, issue, or concern and are asked to recall that Occurrence of Significance, they will likely include a description or explanation of that Occurrence of Significance. Examples of statements that typically have an Occurrence of Significance include descriptions of automobile accidents, injuries, physical altercations, surprises, arguments, or interactions with law enforcement officials.

If someone describes a significant incident, problem, issue, or concern that they experienced and they DON'T include any information about that Occurrence of Significance, it might mean they are strategically withholding guilty knowledge.

Examining a statement's Occurrence of Significance is a two-step process:

STEP 1: Find the Statement's Occurrence of Significance

The part of a statement that I call the Occurrence of Significance starts when the author begins to describe being alerted to an incident, problem, issue, or concern and ends when the author indicates that the incident, problem, issue, or concern has been neutralized or is no longer present.

STEP 2: Calculate the Proportion of the Occurrence of Significance

Once we find a statement's Occurrence of Significance, we need to calculate the size of that occurrence as a proportion of the overall statement. This is a simple math problem:
- First, count the number of words in the statement's Occurrence of Significance;
- Then, count the total number of words in the entire statement;
- Finally, divide the number of words in the Occurrence of Significance by the total number of words in the statement.

This gives you the percentage of the Occurrence of Significance to the entire statement — its proportion of the statement (round your answer to two decimal points for ease of use). For example, a statement's word count is 100 words and its Occurrence of Significance is 50 words– 50 divided by 100 equals .50 or 50 percent. We now know that the Occurrence of Significance is 50 percent of that entire statement.

EXAMPLES

To mark a statement's Occurrence of Significance draw a box around it so you can easily see where it begins and where it ends.

STEP ONE: FIND THE OCCURRENCE OF SIGNIFICANCE

These example statements show how to recognize the Occurrence of Significance. I have drawn a box around the Occurrence of Significance in each statement and followed each with an explanation. Review each one to understand the concept.

Example Statement 1

> "I was walking along the boardwalk when someone grabbed me around the waist and threw me to the ground. I hit the ground hard. I screamed for help and when I did the person ran away and I called the police."

Location of Occurrence of Significance in box:

> "I was walking along the boardwalk when ⟦someone grabbed me around the waist and threw me to the ground. I hit the ground hard. I screamed for help and when I did the person ran away⟧ and I called the police."

Explanation: The Occurrence of Significance begins when the author describes being grabbed (the moment when the statement's author notes the concern) and ends when the author describes the attacker running away (the moment when the concern stops).

Example Statement 2

> "As I was walking across the intersection, I heard a loud car horn to my left. I jumped back and a car slid into my knees. It knocked me into the pavement. The car stopped and the driver asked if I was okay."

Location of Occurrence of Significance in box:

> "As I was walking across the intersection, ⌈I heard a loud car horn to my left. I jumped back and a car slid into my knees. It knocked me into the pavement. The car stopped⌉ and the driver asked if I was okay."

Explanation: The Occurrence of Significance begins when the author describes hearing a loud car horn and ends when the author describes the car stopping.

Example Statement 3

> "I was bringing in my mail when I stepped on what I thought was a stick. Then I felt a horrible pain on my foot. I looked and saw a scorpion on my foot. I jumped up and down until it released and crawled away. I then yelled for my wife to call 911."

Location of Occurrence of Significance in box:

> "I was bringing in my mail when I stepped on what I thought was a stick. ⌈Then I felt a horrible pain on my foot. I looked and saw a scorpion on my foot. I jumped up and down until it released and crawled away.⌉ I then yelled for my wife to call 911."

Explanation: The Occurrence of Significance begins when the author describes feeling a horrible pain–not when the author stepped on something that felt like a stick–and it ends when the author describes the scorpion crawling away.

Chapter 2: Occurrence Of Significance

Example Statement 4

> "As I was watching television, I heard a loud cracking sound and I heard a boom and felt my house shake. I was scared and then my kids came running downstairs and said there was a tree in their bedroom. I got everyone outside where we were safe and called the fire and rescue."

Location of Occurrence of Significance in box:

> "As I was watching television, ⌈I heard a loud cracking sound and I heard a boom and felt my house shake. I was scared and then my kids came running downstairs and said there was a tree in their bedroom. I got everyone outside where we were safe⌋ and called the fire and rescue."

Explanation: The Occurrence of Significance begins when the author hears a loud cracking sound and it ends when the author describes getting everyone to a safe area.

Example Statement 5

> "While I was driving north on Elm a man jumped out of the bushes and threw a red fire extinguisher at my car. It hit my windshield and cracked it. The man then yelled at me and ran south on Elm. I drove home and called you guys."

Location of Occurrence of Significance in box:

> "While I was driving north on Elm ⌈a man jumped out of the bushes and threw a red fire extinguisher at my car. It hit my windshield and cracked it. The man then yelled at me and ran south on Elm.⌋ I drove home and called you guys."

Explanation: The Occurrence of Significance begins when the author describes a man jumping out the bushes and throwing a red fire extinguisher at the car and it ends when the author describes the attacker running away.

Example Statement 6

"At about 5:00 pm I was at my apartment cooking dinner. I had gotten home earlier than usual because I had some friends coming over for dinner. I was cooking lasagna and using a recipe that had been recommended to me by a lady from my support group (Italian Foodies) that meets every Friday night at the recreation center. As I was straining the pasta, I looked out my window and saw a man with a mask walk down the alley located between the back of my building and the back of some businesses on the other side of the alley. He was slightly crouched over and holding a bottle in his right hand with a rag sticking out of it. He walked along the back of the alley and he kept looking over his shoulder like he didn't want anybody to see him. As he crept along, he kept looking at the back of the businesses as if he was looking for a certain one. Eventually he stopped at the back of The Matchstick Lounge and walked up to its back door. He then bent over and lit the rag. After it was lit, he smashed a window beside the door and threw the bottle through it. I then saw a big glow and the man ran away. I picked up my phone and called the police. You guys and the fire department got here a few minutes later."

Chapter 2: Occurrence Of Significance

Location of Occurrence of Significance in box:

> "At about 5:00 pm I was at my apartment cooking dinner. I had gotten home earlier than usual because I had some friends coming over for dinner. I was cooking lasagna and using a recipe that had been recommended to me by a lady from my support group (Italian Foodies) that meets every Friday night at the recreation center. As I was straining the pasta, ⌐I looked out my window and saw a man with a mask walk down the alley located between the back of my building and the back of some businesses on the other side of the alley. He was slightly crouched over and holding a bottle in his right hand with a rag sticking out of it. He walked along the back of the alley and he kept looking over his shoulder like he didn't want anybody to see him. As he crept along, he kept looking at the back of the businesses as if he was looking for a certain one. Eventually he stopped at the back of The Matchstick Lounge and walked up to its back door. He then bent over and lit the rag. After it was lit, he smashed a window beside the door and threw the bottle through it. I then saw a big glow and the man ran away.⌐ I picked up my phone and called the police. You guys and the fire department got here a few minutes later."

Explanation: In this example the Occurrence of Significance starts when the witness describes a man wearing a mask and it ends when the man runs away.

STEP TWO: DETERMINE THE PROPORTION

Below I've used the previous six examples to demonstrate how to calculate the proportion of the Occurrence of Significance.

Example Statement 1

> "I was walking along the boardwalk when someone grabbed me around the waist and threw me to the ground. I hit the ground hard. I screamed for help and when I did the person ran away and I called the police."

Calculation: The Occurrence of Significance is 29 words out of the statement's total of 41 words, meaning about 71 percent of the statement is dedicated to the Occurrence of Significance (29 divided by 41 equals about .71 or 71 percent).

Example Statement 2

> "As I was walking across the intersection, I heard a loud car horn to my left. I jumped back and a car slid into my knees. It knocked me into the pavement. The car stopped and the driver asked if I was okay."

Calculation: The Occurrence of Significance is 28 words of the 43-word statement, or about 65 percent (28 divided by 43 equals about .65 or 65 percent).

Example Statement 3

> "I was bringing in my mail when I stepped on what I thought was a stick. Then I felt a horrible pain on my foot. I looked and saw a scorpion on my foot. I jumped up and down until it released and crawled away. I then yelled for my wife to call 911."

Calculation: The Occurrence of Significance is 29 words of the 54-word statement, or about 54 percent (29 divided by 54 equals about .54 or 54 percent).

Example Statement 4

"As I was watching television, I heard a loud cracking sound and I heard a boom and felt my house shake. I was scared and then my kids came running downstairs and said there was a tree in their bedroom. I got everyone outside where we were safe and called the fire and rescue."

Calculation: The Occurrence of Significance is about 80 percent (43 divided by 54 equals about .80 or 80 percent).

Example Statement 5

"While I was driving north on Elm a man jumped out of the bushes and threw a red fire extinguisher at my car. It hit my windshield and cracked it. The man then yelled at me and ran south on Elm. I drove home and called you guys."

Calculation: The Occurrence of Significance is about 71 percent (34 words divided by 48 words is about .71 or 71 percent).

Example Statement 6

> "At about 5:00 pm I was at my apartment cooking dinner. I had gotten home earlier than usual because I had some friends coming over for dinner. I was cooking lasagna and using a recipe that had been recommended to me by a lady from my support group (Italian Foodies) that meets every Friday night at the recreation center. As I was straining the pasta, I looked out my window and saw a man with a mask walk down the alley located between the back of my building and the back of some businesses on the other side of the alley. He was slightly crouched over and holding a bottle in his right hand with a rag sticking out of it. He walked along the back of the alley and he kept looking over his shoulder like he didn't want anybody to see him. As he crept along, he kept looking at the back of the businesses as if he was looking for a certain one. Eventually he stopped at the back of The Matchstick Lounge and walked up to its back door. He then bent over and lit the rag. After it was lit, he smashed a window beside the door and threw the bottle through it. I then saw a big glow and the man ran away. I picked up my phone and called the police. You guys and the fire department got here a few minutes later."

Calculation: The Occurrence of Significance is 154 words of 240 total words, or about 64 percent of the entire statement (154 divided by 240 is approximately .64 or 64 percent).

Chapter 2: Occurrence Of Significance

PRACTICE EXERCISE

In this practice exercise, **draw a box around the Occurrence of Significance** and then try to **determine its proportion of the overall statement**. The statement concerns a man who says he was robbed outside Dirty Dan's Pool Hall. Don't worry if your answer doesn't exactly match mine–it is understanding the concept that is important.

> "I drove to Dirty Dan's Pool Hall at about 2:30 pm to shoot some pool. I took the Parkway to the Wisdom Road exit. I then took Route 173 over to Myles Boulevard where I stopped at Dixie Chiller and had a hamburger with fries. I was the only person in the restaurant at the time so I decided to take out my wallet to see if I still had the coupon for a free hour of pool at Dirty Dan's. I found it and left. After arriving at Dirty Dan's, I got out of my car, grabbed my pool stick from the back seat, and locked my doors. As I was about to walk away, I felt something in my back and a man told me not to move. He took my wallet and left. After he was gone, I walked around the parking lot to see if he discarded my wallet somewhere nearby. I looked under cars, behind cars, behind the dumpster, in the alley and behind the pool hall. Nothing there. I then went to Dan's and told them what happened and they said they did not see anybody suspicious in the area. I then called the police to tell them what happened and you guys showed up. That's all."

Use this space to calculate the proportion of the Occurrence of Significance to the overall statement: _____

Answer:

> "I drove to Dirty Dan's Pool Hall at about 2:30 pm to shoot some pool. I took the Parkway to the Wisdom Road exit. I then took Route 173 over to Myles Boulevard where I stopped at Dixie Chiller and had a hamburger with fries. I was the only person in the restaurant at the time so I decided to take out my wallet to see if I still had the coupon for a free hour of pool at Dirty Dan's. I found it and left. After arriving at Dirty Dan's, I got out of my car, grabbed my pool stick from the back seat, and locked my doors. As I was about to walk away, ⟦I felt something in my back and a man told me not to move. He took my wallet and left.⟧ After he was gone, I walked around the parking lot to see if he discarded my wallet somewhere nearby. I looked under cars, behind cars, behind the dumpster, in the alley and behind the pool hall. Nothing there. I then went to Dan's and told them what happened and they said they did not see anybody suspicious in the area. I then called the police to tell them what happened and you guys showed up. That's all."

Explanation: The Occurrence of Significance starts when the victim says he felt an object in his back and ends when the robber leaves the area.

Calculation: In this case the Occurrence of Significance is 20 words out of the overall statement of 214 words or about 9 percent (20 divided by 214 is about .09 or 9 percent of the entire statement).

OCCURRENCE OF SIGNIFICANCE & COMMITMENT

The Occurrence of Significance provides meaning to a statement. A statement that does not have an Occurrence of Significance is like a mystery novel without a crime. It has a beginning and an ending, but no middle. It simply does not make sense.

Because the Occurrence of Significance is crucial to statements, it follows that it will likely be a substantial part of the statement. A statement examiner should feel more comfortable with statements in which the Occurrence of Significance is a large percentage of the entire statement and less comfortable with statements in which the Occurrence of Significance is a smaller percentage. As a general rule, a statement with a larger Occurrence of Significance reflects an author with a high level of commitment to the statement, and a statement with a smaller Occurrence of Significance, 33 percent or lower, or no Occurrence of Significance, reflects an author with a low level of commitment to the statement.

In the sample statement about the firebombing at the Matchstick Lounge, the examiner should be comfortable with the size of the Occurrence of Significance (64 percent) as it indicates the author has a substantial commitment to the significant incident.

Conversely, in the exercise example involving the robbery outside Dirty Dan's Pool Hall, the reviewer should be uncomfortable with the small proportion of the Occurrence of Significance (at only 9 percent). The Occurrence of Significance–a significant incident, problem, issue, or concern (such as being robbed)–should be larger than 9 percent of the overall statement. The statement examiner should consider the possibility that the victim minimized the Occurrence of Significance to avoid exposing guilty knowledge.

PLEASE NOTE

A statement examiner should not conclude that a small Occurrence of Significance of less than 33 percent is always an indicator that someone is withholding guilty knowledge. It is simply an indicator that someone may be withholding guilty knowledge. In my experience I have examined some statements containing a small Occurrence of Significance that later turned out to be true. It typically doesn't happen, but it occasionally does. Some reasons why a truthful author might provide a statement with a small Occurrence of Significance are that they don't feel comfortable discussing what happened, that they don't understand the interviewer's question, or that they feel traumatized by the incident and therefore don't have the ability to recall everything that happened.

PRACTICE EXERCISES

In each of these statements, **draw a box around the Occurrence of Significance**, **determine its proportion** compared to the overall statement, and then **decide if the statement's author appears committed to the statement**.

EXERCISE 1

> "As I walked out of the restaurant, I noticed a man walking toward me and carrying a broomstick. We made eye contact, he held the broomstick over his head, yelled a curse word, and began running in my direction. I immediately ran back into the restaurant and grabbed a big waiter. The man followed me into the restaurant, and when he saw the waiter he yelled more curse words at me, turned, and ran away. I then called 911."

Use this space to calculate the proportion of the Occurrence of Significance to the overall statement: _____

Answer:

> "As I walked out of the restaurant, I noticed a man walking toward me and carrying a broomstick. We made eye contact, ⌈he held the broomstick over his head, yelled a curse word, and began running in my direction. I immediately ran back into the restaurant and grabbed a big waiter. The man followed me into the restaurant, and when he saw the waiter he yelled more curse words at me, turned, and ran away.⌋ I then called 911."

Explanation: The Occurrence of Significance begins when the victim perceives the threat, at the moment the man places the broomstick over his head, not when the victim first notices the man or makes eye contact with him. It ends when the man runs out of the restaurant.

Calculation: The victim's statement uses 79 words to describe the entire incident and 53 to describe the Occurrence of Significance or approximately 67 percent of the entire statement. This percentage is consistent with someone committed to their statement.

Chapter 2: Occurrence Of Significance

EXERCISE 2

Here is the same statement but with a small change to the Occurrence of Significance. **Draw a box around the Occurrence of Significance, determine its proportion** compared to the overall statement, and then **decide if the statement's author appears committed to the statement**.

> "As I walked out of the restaurant, I noticed a man walking toward me and carrying a broomstick. As he walked by me, he hit my shoulder twice with the broomstick. I fell to the ground and then he kicked my leg and took my phone. At that point a waiter ran out of the restaurant and the man attacking me ran away. The waiter then called 911."

Use this space to calculate the proportion of the Occurrence of Significance to the overall statement: _____

Answer:

> "As I walked out of the restaurant, I noticed a man walking toward me and carrying a broomstick. As he walked by me, |he hit my shoulder twice with the broomstick. I fell to the ground and then he kicked my leg and took my phone. At that point a waiter ran out of the restaurant and the man attacking me ran away.| The waiter then called 911."

Explanation: The Occurrence of Significance starts when the subject walks by her and hits her twice on the shoulder–the victim perceives the threat at that point, not when the victim first notices him or sees him simply carrying a broomstick–and it ends when the man flees.

Calculation: The victim uses 68 words to describe the entire incident and 40 words to describe the Occurrence of Significance. The victim's statement has an Occurrence of Significance of approximately 59 percent of the overall statement, likely consistent with someone committed to their story.

EXERCISE 3

Same statement again, with another change. **Draw a box around the Occurrence of Significance, determine its proportion** compared to the overall statement, and then **decide if the statement's author appears committed to the statement**.

> "As I walked out of the restaurant – I had just finished a plate of lasagna with a big dessert and was extremely full at this point – someone hit me and ran away. They probably made a left on Main Street and went into the abandoned buildings. I didn't get a good look at them but it was probably a man. I walked into the restaurant and told them what happened. They called the cops."

Use this space to calculate the proportion of the Occurrence of Significance to the overall statement: _____

Answer:

> "As I walked out of the restaurant – I had just finished a plate of lasagna with a big dessert and was extremely full at this point – [someone hit me and ran away.] They probably made a left on Main Street and went into the abandoned buildings. I didn't get a good look at them but it was probably a man. I walked into the restaurant and told them what happened. They called the cops."

Explanation: The Occurrence of Significance starts when the victim is hit and ends when the assailant runs away.

Calculation: The victim uses 74 words to describe the entire incident and six words to describe the Occurrence of Significance–approximately 8 percent of the overall statement. This person is likely not committed to their statement.

TIPS

TIP 1 **DON'T ASSUME ALL STATEMENTS HAVE AN OCCURRENCE OF SIGNIFICANCE**

Whether or not a statement contains an Occurrence of Significance depends on the witness's experience. If someone witnesses a significant incident, problem, issue, or concern, their statement will probably have an Occurrence of Significance. But logically, if they did NOT witness a significant incident, problem, issue, or concern then it is unlikely their statement will have an Occurrence of Significance.

To illustrate: If a fireman saw someone walking a dog down the street where a dumpster fire had just occurred, he might ask, "What happened?" If the person did not see anything of significance, they may reply, "I was walking my dog and I just got here. I didn't see anything." Unfortunately, this potential witness did not see anything and therefore did not have an Occurrence of Significance to report.

TIP 2 **USE OPEN-ENDED QUESTIONS**

One of the most effective ways to get someone to provide a statement with an Occurrence of Significance is to ask them an open-ended question such as: "Can you tell me what happened?" By asking this question, the interviewer minimizes the chances of leading their subject and thus contaminating the statement.

CHAPTER 3: HIGH-QUALITY SENSORY DETAILS

This chapter examines High-Quality Sensory Details and answers these questions:
• What is a High-Quality Sensory Detail?
• How do we recognize High-Quality Sensory Details?
• What do High-Quality Sensory Details tell us about an author's commitment to their statement?

Before diving into this chapter, I'd like for you take a moment to write down an important event that you remember from your childhood. Write what happened below or use the blank NOTES pages at the back of this book. Please write your response before continuing with this chapter.

Write here:

> *"Details make perfection, and perfection is not a detail."*
>
> – Leonardo Da Vinci

Now that you've written down your memory, here is a memory that I have from 55 years ago:

> *"I was in second grade and playing a game called maul ball during recess. On this day Joe had the ball and was being chased by my classmates and me. Joe was eventually caught and threw the ball away ... to me. I caught the ball and was about to run when I saw Steve throw something at me. He was standing by himself at the far end of the playground beside the gray steel monkey bars when he threw it. I remember it being brown and oblong; it looked like a small brown potato and it was traveling directly toward me. Instead of running or ducking, I continued to watch the object fly toward my head. When it made impact, I realized it was rock! My head had been hit by a rock and I began to cry.*
>
> *I was hurt, bleeding, and scared. I stood there holding the ball and after several seconds I felt two arms reach out and grab me. It was a teacher. She carried me to the principal's office where I was safe. The principal got some wet, brown paper towels and placed them on my head. When he couldn't stop the bleeding, he told the vice principal to call my mother. She arrived a few minutes later and took me to the local hospital where I received two stitches above my eye. I then went home."*

What was the purpose of this exercise–other than to highlight my age? It shows how most people naturally recall, in detail, important events that happened from many years ago. Research tells us that we have three types of long-term memory (McLeod, 2023):

- Procedural Memory: specific procedures such as driving a car or riding a bicycle;
- Semantic Memory: facts such as knowing the name of the first president or the U.S. capital;
- Episodic Memory: significant life events.

When I wrote about the important event from my childhood, I used my episodic memory, and you likely used your episodic memory when you wrote about your own childhood memory. My personal childhood recollection has many details, some of which are High-Quality Sensory Details. High-Quality Sensory Details are specific details captured through our senses and stored in our long-term memory. These details often show an author's commitment to what they are saying and are good indicators of veracity in the part of the statement where those details are located.

SCALE OF DETAIL

To understand how to recognize High-Quality Sensory Details, think of a horizontal scale that starts at 0 and ends at 10–we'll call this the scale of detail. Zero on the scale means there is no detail and 10 means there is a high-level of detail. For details to qualify as High-

Quality Sensory Details, they should land between 8 and 10 on the scale.

If I am asked to describe what is covering my feet, I might say *shoes*, and that would be a detail; not much of a detail, but still a detail and would score a 2 on the scale of detail. If I describe those things on my feet as *brown shoes*. I would give this description a score of 5 on the scale of detail–it's a good detail but doesn't meet the level of description necessary to qualify as a High-Quality Sensory Detail. A lot of brown shoes exist! If I describe those things on my feet as *brown suede shoes,* I would give the description an 8 on the scale of detail and consider it a High-Quality Sensory Detail. If I add the detail *blue shoestrings* then the description would likely reach 9 or 10.

Another example: If I describe my water container as a *bottle,* I would score the detail as a 1 or 2 on the scale of detail. Maybe I describe my water container as a *plastic bottle*. In this case I would give the description a score of 4 or 5 on the scale of detail–a good description, but still lacking the detail necessary to qualify as a High-Quality Sensory Detail. Suppose I describe the water container as a *plastic bottle with a red cap*. In this case I would score the level of detail at an 8 on the scale of detail. In my opinion it qualifies as a High-Quality Sensory Detail. If I had included the detail of a *green label*, my score would have probably gone up to 9 or 10.

EXAMPLES

Underline any High-Quality Sensory Details you find in a statement.

Question	Low-Quality Sensory Detail	High-Quality Sensory Detail
What did he drive?	He drove a car.	He drove a <u>blue convertible with ruby-red racing stripes</u>.
What did the playing field look like?	It was green.	It was <u>green with blue artificial turf in its end zones</u>.
What did you see at the theater?	A movie.	We saw <u>The Man With Seven Eyes</u>.
Can you describe the house's chimney?	Yes, it was made of bricks.	Yes, it was <u>round with algae on its bricks</u>.
Why are you limping?	I hurt myself.	A baseball hit <u>my left kneecap</u>.
What did the tornado sound like?	It was a loud noise.	It sounded like a <u>locomotive rolling down the tracks</u>.
What was he wearing when he did it?	He was wearing something orange.	He was wearing <u>orange coveralls with the letters "LJ" on the bib</u>.
What did the chef's special taste like?	It tasted horrible.	It <u>tasted like hot vinegar</u>.
Why did you change lockers?	My old locker smelled.	My old locker <u>smelled like a dirty aquarium</u>.
Did the explosion hurt you?	Yes, it hurt me.	It left <u>blisters inside my nostrils</u>.
What do you remember about him?	He had a tattoo.	He had a <u>green tattoo of a shark on his upper back</u>.

Example Statement

Take a look again at my childhood memory. Do you see any High-Quality Sensory Details?

> "I was in second grade and playing a game called maul ball during recess. On this day Joe had the ball and was being chased by my classmates and me. Joe was eventually caught and threw the ball away ... to me. I caught the ball and was about to run when I saw Steve throw something at me. He was standing by himself at the far end of the playground beside the gray steel monkey bars when he threw it. I remember it being brown and oblong; it looked like a small brown potato and it was traveling directly toward me. Instead of running or ducking, I continued to watch the object fly toward my head. When it made impact, I realized it was rock! My head had been hit by a rock and I began to cry.
>
> I was hurt, bleeding, and scared. I stood there holding the ball and after several seconds I felt two arms reach out and grab me. It was a teacher. She carried me to the principal's office where I was safe. The principal got some wet, brown paper towels and placed them on my head. When he couldn't stop the bleeding, he told the vice principal to call my mother. She arrived a few minutes later and took me to the local hospital where I received two stitches above my eye. I then went home."

High-Quality Sensory Details underlined.

> "I was in second grade and playing a game called maul ball during recess. On this day Joe had the ball and was being chased by my classmates and me. Joe was eventually caught and threw the ball away ... to me. I caught the ball and was about to run when I saw Steve throw something at me. He was standing by himself at the far end of the playground beside the <u>gray steel monkey bars</u> when he threw it. I remember it being <u>brown and oblong</u>; it looked like a <u>small brown potato</u> and it was traveling directly toward me. Instead of running or ducking, I continued to watch the object fly toward my head. When it made impact, I realized it was rock! My head had been hit by a rock and I began to cry.
>
> I was hurt, bleeding, and scared. I stood there holding the ball and after several seconds I felt two arms reach out and grab me. It was a teacher. She carried me to the principal's office where I was safe. The principal got some <u>wet, brown paper towels</u> and placed them on my head. When he couldn't stop the bleeding, he told the vice principal to call my mother. She arrived a few minutes later and took me to the local hospital where I received <u>two stitches above my eye</u>. I then went home."

Take a moment to go back and look at your own childhood memory? What High-Quality Sensory Details can you find?

PRACTICE EXERCISES

EXERCISE 1

This statement is from a man who had an accident while at work and is asked to explain what happened. **Underline any High-Quality Sensory Details** you find in his statement.

> "I got to work and was setting up the saw as I normally do. About a minute into the cutting, one of the blades broke and it cut me from the base of my right palm to the top of my pinkie finger. I wrapped my hand in a rag and told my supervisor. He called an ambulance."

Answer:

> "I got to work and was setting up the saw as I normally do. About a minute into the cutting, one of the blades broke and it cut me from the <u>base of my right palm to the top of my pinkie finger.</u> I wrapped my hand in a rag and told my supervisor. He called an ambulance."

Explanation: The author's description of his injury shows a high level of commitment.

EXERCISE 2

This statement is from a woman who says she was injured during a fall in a retail department store. **Underline any High-Quality Sensory Details**.

> "I went to Slipp's Department Store to buy something as I usually do when I have extra money on the weekend. I walked down several aisles and didn't find anything. I then walked around some more and when I couldn't find what I was looking for, I decided to leave. I looked for about 30 minutes. As I was leaving the store, I slipped and started to fall. I then hit the floor and yelled for help. A manager ran over and picked me up. He asked if I was okay and I said I wasn't. He asked if I was hurt and told him yes. He asked where I was hurt, and I told him I thought I was hurt about my body."

Answer:

This statement contains no High-Quality Sensory Details. The author has an excellent opportunity to give such details when asked to explain where she was hurt, but instead she says, "I thought I was hurt about my body." Where's the commitment? "About my body" could be any part of her body. Why didn't she give a specific location of her injury? Perhaps she thought that a detailed description of her injury would cause her embarrassment (maybe she injured a private part) or maybe she gave an intentionally vague description because she was not hurt.

If the important memory from your childhood that you wrote at the start of this chapter involved an injury, you likely gave details about the location of that injury. My guess is you didn't claim you were hurt "about your body." Is the author definitely lying in this case? Perhaps. What we do know is the author appears to lack commitment regarding her injury. To determine why she appears to lack commitment, she should be re-interviewed and given the opportunity to offer a response with a more detailed description of her injury, if she can.

EXERCISE 3

This statement is from a young man whose parents ask him to explain what he did between noon and dinner. **Underline any High-Quality Sensory Details** in the son's response.

> "I went to Kenny's house at noon and we played basketball in his backyard. His father just installed a new basketball hoop. It's an SSV model with an adjustable height mechanism that allows it to be adjusted between seven and ten feet. We played on it until it was time for me to make my way home for dinner. On the way home I walked through the park and saw some boys playing touch football with a soft orange football. They asked me to play and I said I couldn't because I had to go home and eat dinner."

Answer:

> "I went to Kenny's house at noon and we played basketball in his backyard. His father just installed a new basketball hoop. It's an <u>SSV model with an adjustable height mechanism that allows it to be adjusted between seven and ten feet</u>. We played on it until it was time for me to make my way home for dinner. On the way home I walked through the park and saw some boys playing touch football with a <u>soft orange football</u>. They asked me to play and I said I couldn't because I had to go home and eat dinner."

Explanation: The description of the basketball hoop and of the other boys' football are High-Quality Sensory Details.

EXERCISE 4

This statement is from a man who discovered a fire. **Underline any High-Quality Sensory Details**.

> "I came into the restaurant at 2:00 pm as I usually do. I then started setting up the tables. When I was finished, I went downstairs to get some more linens and that is when I smelled something bad like burning rubber. I traced the smell and eventually determined it was coming from the dryer. I saw some black smoke lifting up from behind the dryer and then I saw some flames shoot up from behind the dryer also. I yelled, "fire." Paul came downstairs and called the fire department. By now the flames were covering the wall and black smoke stung my eyes and choked me. We then went outside and waited."

Answer:

> "I came into the restaurant at 2:00 pm as I usually do. I then started setting up the tables. When I was finished, I went downstairs to get some more linens and that is when I <u>smelled something bad like burning rubber</u>. I traced the smell and eventually determined it was coming from the dryer. <u>I saw some black smoke lifting up from behind the dryer</u> and then <u>I saw some flames shoot up from behind the dryer</u> also. I yelled, "fire." Paul came downstairs and called the fire department. By now the <u>flames were covering the wall</u> and <u>black smoke stung my eyes and choked me</u>. We then went outside and waited."

Explanation: The smell of burning rubber, the visual description of smoke and flames, and the physical impact the smoke had on the author are all High-Quality Sensory Details, indicating that the author is likely committed to those parts of the statement.

EXERCISE 5

Underline any High-Quality Sensory Details in this statement from a man who injured himself.

> "On Halloween I arrived at the gym at 4:30. I immediately went to the desk and gave Rachael my ID and she scanned it for me. She was wearing a white nurses' outfit from like the 60s or 70s with a white bonnet and stethoscope. After she scanned me in, I went the locker room and got dressed. Today was an upper body day so I decided to concentrate on my arms, chest and back. I stretched for a few minutes and then went to the bench and started my bench press routine. It went fine. I then started on my arms and was on my third set and lowering the bar to my waist when I heard a loud 'pop' sound and felt this burning pain coming from my right bicep. I immediately dropped the bar and sat down. I looked at my right arm and my bicep was now a fat knot and looked like a misshapen ball of clay. I went to the front desk and they called an ambulance and put ice on my arm."

Answer:

> "On Halloween I arrived at the gym at 4:30. I immediately went to the desk and gave Rachael my ID and she scanned it for me. She was wearing <u>a white nurses' outfit from like the 60s or 70s with a white bonnet and stethoscope</u>. After she scanned me in, I went the locker room and got dressed. Today was an upper body day so I decided to concentrate on my arms, chest and back. I stretched for a few minutes and then went to the bench and started my bench press routine. It went fine. I then started on my arms and was on my third set and lowering the bar to my waist <u>when I heard a loud 'pop' sound and felt this burning pain coming from my right bicep</u>. I immediately dropped the bar and sat down. I looked at my right arm and <u>my bicep was now a fat knot and looked like a misshapen ball of clay</u>. I went to the front desk and they called an ambulance and put ice on my arm."

Explanation: The author's description of the nurse's uniform, the "pop" sound, the burning pain in the right arm, and his misshapen arm are all High-Quality Sensory Details.

TIPS

TIP 1 — ASK QUESTIONS

If you agree with the following three questions then you likely have found High-Quality Sensory Details:
- Do you agree that the word(s) paint a picture in your mind?
- Do you agree that the word(s) reflect a high level of sensory detail?
- Do you agree that someone hiding guilty information would NOT provide this much detail?

TIP 2 — DON'T ASSUME HIGH-QUALITY SENSORY DETAILS ALWAYS INDICATE TRUTHFULNESS

If someone gives a statement with High-Quality Sensory Details, that does not always indicate they are telling the truth. It is possible they may be manipulating reality. Authors of fictional statements may use a strategy I refer to as incident masking in which the person mentally accesses details from a previous incident in their lives and substitutes those details for reality in their current statement. This strategy can be effective and provide artificial details. As an example, if I am involved in a hit-and-run car accident and I tell the detective I wasn't involved because I was at the park walking my dog at the time, I could use details from a previous outing to the park to convince the investigator of my alibi.

TIP 3 — LOCATION OF HIGH-QUALITY DETAILS IS IMPORTANT

High-Quality Sensory Details can be found anywhere in a statement. They typically indicate an author's commitment to that particular part of the statement. I find it especially useful to find those details in and around the Occurrence of Significance—the area where an author expresses their problem, issue, or concern.

TIP 4 — NOT ALL TRUE STATEMENTS HAVE HIGH-QUALITY SENSORY DETAILS

Some statements do not have High-Quality Sensory Details. Does this mean the author is trying to avoid exposing guilty knowledge? No, some people simply do not provide them in their statements.

TIP 5 — NOT GIVING HIGH-QUALITY SENSORY DETAILS AVOIDS CORROBORATION

Authors who want to avoid exposing their guilty knowledge may not provide many High-Quality Sensory Details in their statement because curious people may try to corroborate or verify those details, and in the process expose the truth.

CHAPTER 4: HIGH-QUALITY LOCATIONAL DETAILS

This chapter examines High-Quality Locational Details and answers these questions:
• What are High-Quality Locational Details?
• How do we recognize High-Quality Locational Details in a statement?
• What do High-Quality Locational Details tell us about an author's commitment to their statement?

Much like High-Quality Sensory Details discussed in the previous chapter, High-Quality Locational Details are specific details, but these details describe locations. High-Quality Locational Details show an author's commitment to that part of the statement in which the details are located and are a possible indicator of veracity.

If someone describes their favorite hiding place as "behind my house," the phrase "behind my house" is a locational detail. It's not much of a detail but it is a locational detail. For it to be considered a High-Quality Locational Detail the phrase needs a higher level of detail. By adding "under the oak tree" or "10 feet north of the swing set" to the phrase "behind my house" it becomes a High-Quality Locational Detail.

SCALE OF DETAIL

To recognize High-Quality Locational Details we again use the scale of detail. Zero on the scale represents no detail and 10 represents a high level of detail. For a detail to be a High-Quality Locational Detail it should be between 8 and 10 on the scale.

> "If you tell the truth, you don't have to remember anything."
> – Mark Twain

Suppose I'm asked to describe where I live and I say I live in Virginia. That is a locational detail, but not much of one and would score a 2 on the scale of detail. If I say I live on Veracity Lane in Virginia, that would score a 5 or 6 on the scale—it's a good detail but because there are many houses located on that street the location doesn't meet the level of detail necessary to qualify as a High-Quality Locational Detail.

If I say my house is across the street from Big Lick's Ice Cream Factory on Veracity Lane in Virginia this would score an 8 and be considered a High-Quality Locational Detail. If I say my house is at 12300 Veracity Lane, Virginia, across the street from Big Lick's Ice Cream Factory, then it is a 10. Another example: If I am asked to describe where I parked my car when I went shopping and I say I parked my car at the mall, this locational detail would score about a 2 or 3 on the scale. If I say I parked behind the mall, this is more specific but still would not qualify as a High-Quality Locational Detail and is around a 5 on the scale. If I say I parked next to the spa behind the mall, then it scores a 9 or 10.

EXAMPLES

Underline any High-Quality Locational Details you find in a statement.

Question	Low-Quality Locational Detail	High-Quality Locational Detail
Where was he hiding?	In the house.	Inside the closet in Mike's bedroom.
Where was the party?	In a field.	It was behind the silo at Hank's farm.
Where did you sit?	In the theater.	In the third row in front of the orchestra pit.
Where did you go last night?	To the beach.	To Blob's Beach at the 17th Street pier.
Where did you find the money?	In the house.	Under the middle sofa cushion in the living room.
Where were you?	I was in the car.	I sat in the back seat of the car, behind the passenger seat.
Where did you see him?	He was in the condo.	He was in the condo, behind the stairwell next to the kitchen.
Where did you leave your sister?	At a restaurant.	On the beach in front of Cooper's Sushi House.
Where does she live?	She lives in Maryland.	She lives at 5589 Elmwood Road in Clydesville, Maryland.
Where did you last see her?	She was at the park.	She was at E Street Park, about two miles south of the tracks on Route 7.
Where is the lifeguard stand?	On the beach.	It's on the beach between 120th and 122nd Streets.
Where did you leave the keys?	Someplace in the hotel room.	On the bathroom counter next to the deodorant.
Where did he run?	He ran down the road.	He ran south on Main Street and turned left into Maples Park.
Where did you meet him?	We met downtown.	We met at the escalator located at the entrance to city hall

PRACTICE EXERCISES

EXERCISE 1

This statement is from a woman who says she was robbed. **Underline any High-Quality Locational Details**.

> "I had just finished my math class and was walking across the campus to go to my next class. It was a very windy and gray day in January with snow flurries. As I walked by the north entrance gate to the stadium, I became scared because I heard some loud footsteps running up behind me. I looked over my shoulder and noticed a tall man with a furry brown and white parka running fast in my direction. As I moved to the side, he knocked me to the ground and I hit the pavement hard. I landed between the curb and the front bumper of a truck. My glasses flew off my face and my chin dug into the curb. I then felt the parka man tug at my backpack and rip it away from my body. I didn't move the whole time. Once he had my backpack he ran away and then I called the campus police."

Answer:

> "I had just finished my math class and was walking across the campus to go to my next class. It was a very windy and gray day in January with snow flurries. As I walked by the <u>north entrance gate to the stadium</u>, I became scared because I heard some loud footsteps running up behind me. I looked over my shoulder and noticed a tall man with a furry brown and white parka running fast in my direction. As I moved to the side, he knocked me to the ground and I hit the pavement hard. I landed <u>between the curb and the front bumper of a truck</u>. My glasses flew off my face and my chin dug into the curb. I then felt the parka man tug at my backpack and rip it away from my body. I didn't move the whole time. Once he had my backpack he ran away and then I called the campus police."

Explanation: These details show commitment to her statement. Did you find any High-Quality Sensory Details?

EXERCISE 2

This statement is from a young man who says he was the victim of an attempted kidnapping. **Underline his statement's High-Quality Locational Details.**

"I went to <u>the park</u> to play basketball with my friends on <u>court three at Johnson Rec Center</u>. While we were playing a man standing close to the court started staring at me. He was about 40 and wore a blue hoodie. He stared at me the entire time we were there. I just figured he was a creeper. When the game was over, I started walking home by myself. The creeper got in an old blue car with a cracked window and followed me. I was scared. As I walked in front of <u>the bus stop on 5th and Bloom</u>, he pulled up beside me and asked if I wanted a ride. I said no. He kept asking me over and over and I just ignored him. Finally, he said my mom had an emergency and sent him to pick me up. I ignored him and he started to yell at me to get in the car. When I got to <u>the vacant parking lot on 2nd Street</u>, I ran. He drove up, got out of his car and chased me as I ran to <u>a metal chain-link fence</u> and climbed over. He couldn't make it over and stopped. I ran straight home and my mom called the police."

Answer:

> "I went to the park to play basketball with my friends on <u>court three at Johnson Rec Center</u>. While we were playing a man standing close to the court started staring at me. He was about 40 and wore a blue hoodie. He stared at me the entire time we were there. I just figured he was a creeper. When the game was over, I started walking home by myself. The creeper got in an old blue car with a cracked window and followed me. I was scared. As I walked in front of the <u>bus stop on 5th and Bloom</u>, he pulled up beside me and asked if I wanted a ride. I said no. He kept asking me over and over and I just ignored him. Finally, he said my mom had an emergency and sent him to pick me up. I ignored him and he started to yell at me to get in the car. When I got to the <u>vacant parking lot on 2nd Street,</u> I ran. He drove up, got out of his car and chased me as I ran to a metal chain-link fence and climbed over. He couldn't make it over and stopped. I ran straight home and my mom called the police."

Explanation: The young man provides many High-Quality Locational Details showing his commitment to his statement. Did you also find any High-Quality Sensory Details?

TIPS

TIP 1 — ASK QUESTIONS

If you agree with the following three questions then you likely have found High-Quality Locational Details:

- Do you agree that the word(s) paint a picture in your mind?
- Do you agree that the word(s) reflect a detailed location?
- Do you agree that someone protecting guilty information would NOT provide such a detail?

TIP 2 — DON'T ASSUME HIGH-QUALITY LOCATIONAL DETAILS ALWAYS INDICATE TRUTHFULNESS

If someone provides High-Quality Locational Details in their statement that doesn't necessarily indicate that they are telling the truth. It is still possible they may provide false information through incident masking–mentally accessing detailed information from a previous unrelated incident in their life and then substituting that information as reality in their current response. This is an effective technique for believably inserting false details into a statement.

For example, if I was involved in a theft and I told the interviewing detective I was not involved in the theft because, "I was at Doodle Dan's Theatre at the time of the theft." If the detective asked me to explain what I did there, I could simply tell the detective about a previous trip I had made a week earlier; using the details from that earlier trip as part of my current alibi.

TIP 3 — LOOK FOR HIGH-QUALITY LOCATIONAL DETAILS NEAR THE OCCURRENCE OF SIGNIFICANCE

High-Quality Locational Details can be found anywhere in a statement, but it is preferable to find them in and around the Occurrence of Significance. That is the place where the author is likely to express details about their problem, issue, or concern.

TIP 4 — SOME TRUTHFUL STATEMENTS MAY NOT CONTAIN HIGH-QUALITY LOCATIONAL DETAILS

Some statements do not have High-Quality Locational Details because some people simply do not provide them in their statements. Although High-Quality Locational Details are good indicators of commitment, the examiner should never conclude that someone is hiding guilty information simply because they don't provide these details in their statement.

COMPREHENSIVE EXERCISE 1

This exercise uses the following statement to practice finding all the methodologies covered so far. This statement is from a woman who witnessed an automobile accident.

> "I was driving over the Route 81 bridge headed east at mile marker 38, when suddenly a dark blue dump truck moved into the right lane and cut off a pick-up truck. The pick-up truck hit the side of the bridge and actually made its way over the guard rail. I stopped my car and ran back and looked over the bridge. I saw the truck slowly dip lower and lower into the river. When it was almost totally submerged, I dove into the river to help. The water was icy cold and took my breath away. When I was about 10 feet from the driver's front door of the truck, I saw the driver pop up out of the water and ask for help. He was flopping around and I grabbed him. I asked if there was anyone else in the truck and he said no. I had a hard time keeping both of us from going under and we started to sink into the river. I don't know who, but someone threw a spare tire over the bridge. It landed near us and we grabbed it and made our way to the end of the pier on the west shore. An ambulance took us to the hospital where we got checked out."

Steps

1. Draw a box around the Occurrence of Significance.
   Calculate the proportion of the Occurrence of Significance here:

2. Underline any High-Quality Sensory Details.

3. Underline any High-Quality Locational Details.

(Turn page for answers.)

ANSWERS

Occurrence of Significance

> "I was driving over the Route 81 bridge headed east at mile marker 38, when |suddenly a dark blue dump truck moved into the right lane and cut off a pick-up truck. The pick-up truck hit the side of the bridge and actually made its way over the guard rail. I stopped my car and ran back and looked over the bridge. I saw the truck slowly dip lower and lower into the river. When it was almost totally submerged, I dove into the river to help. The water was icy cold and took my breath away. When I was about 10 feet from the driver's front door of the truck, I saw the driver pop up out of the water and ask for help. He was flopping around and I grabbed him. I asked if there was anyone else in the truck and he said no. I had a hard time keeping both of us from going under and we started to sink into the river. I don't know who, but someone threw a spare tire over the bridge. It landed near us and we grabbed it and made our way to the end of the pier on the west shore.| An ambulance took us to the hospital where we got checked out."

Explanation: The Occurrence of Significance begins when the author sees the dump truck cut off the pick-up truck and ends when the driver swims to the pier. The Occurrence of Significance is more than 85 percent of the statement and shows a high level of commitment.

High-Quality Sensory Details

> "I was driving over the Route 81 bridge headed east at mile marker 38, when suddenly a <u>dark blue dump truck</u> moved into the right lane and cut off a pick-up truck. The pick-up truck hit the side of the bridge and actually made its way over the guard rail. I stopped my car and ran back and looked over the bridge. I saw the truck <u>slowly dip lower and lower into the river.</u> When it was almost totally submerged, I dove into the river to help. The <u>water was icy cold and took my breath away</u>. When I was about 10 feet from the driver's front door of the truck, I saw the driver pop up out of the water and ask for help. He was flopping around and I grabbed him. I asked if there was anyone else in the truck and he said no. I had a hard time keeping both of us from going under and we started to sink into the river. I don't know who, but someone threw a spare tire over the bridge. It landed near us and we grabbed it and made our way to the end of the pier on the west shore. An ambulance took us to the hospital where we got checked out."

Explanation: These High-Quality Sensory Details indicate commitment to the statement.

High-Quality Locational Details

> "I was driving over the Route 81 bridge headed east at mile marker 38, when suddenly a <u>dark blue dump truck</u> moved into the right lane and cut off a pick-up truck. The pick-up truck hit the side of the bridge and actually made its way over the guard rail. I stopped my car and ran back and looked over the bridge. I saw the truck <u>slowly dip lower and lower into the river.</u> When it was almost totally submerged, I dove into the river to help. The <u>water was icy cold and took my breath away.</u> When I was about <u>10 feet from the driver's front door of the truck,</u> I saw the driver pop up out of the water and ask for help. He was flopping around and I grabbed him. I asked if there was anyone else in the truck and he said no. I had a hard time keeping both of us from going under and we started to sink into the river. I don't know who, but someone threw a spare tire over the bridge. It landed near us and we grabbed it and made our way to the <u>end of the pier on the west shore.</u> An ambulance took us to the hospital where we got checked out."

Explanation: The High-Quality Locational Details indicate a high level of location specificity.

IMPORTANT NOTE

Your results may not look exactly like mine. That's okay. What's important is if your interpretation of the results indicates the author's commitment or non-commitment to the statement.

CHAPTER 5: PIVOT WORDS

This chapter examines Pivot Words and answers these questions:
- What are Pivot Words?
- How do we recognize Pivot Words in a statement?
- What do Pivot Words tell us about an author's commitment to their statement?

In Chapters 3 and 4 we learned that High-Quality Sensory Details and High-Quality Locational Details indicate an author's commitment and could be indicators of veracity. In this chapter we explore how people use Pivot Words to avoid commitment to their statement and engage in possible deception. Pivot Words can be a single word or a group of words.

WHAT ARE PIVOT WORDS?

People with guilty knowledge who are asked a question that threatens to expose that guilty knowledge will often use Pivot Words to *pivot* from commitment in their statements. A good analogy of this is a basketball player who finds himself surrounded by opposing players, causing the player to stop dribbling. At that point — because the game's rules say the player cannot begin dribbling the ball again — the attacking defense tries to steal the ball or to knock it away. Although the player's situation seems dire, the player still has a chance. According to the rules, the player can rotate away from the

> *"Tricks and treachery are the practice of fools that don't have brains enough to be honest."*
>
> *– Benjamin Franklin*

attacking defense as long as the player keeps one foot (the *pivot* foot) planted on the floor. By using this strategy, the player can avoid the defense until the player can safely shoot the ball or pass the ball to another teammate.

Keeping this analogy in mind, imagine that after a hit-and-run car accident investigators ask a suspect where he was at that time of the accident. If the suspect says, "I was probably at Five Zebras and Burgers," the suspect may have used the Pivot Word *probably* to pivot away from the troublesome question.

If the follow-up investigation determines that the suspect was never at Five Zebras and Burgers and the investigator then confronts the suspect about lying, the suspect can simply refute that allegation. He can say that he never lied because he never said he was *definitely* at Five Zebras and Burgers, but that he said he was *probably* at Five Zebras and Burgers. He could then pivot again and say that if he was not at Five Zebras and Burgers then he was likely at home at the time of the incident. Again, the author uses a Pivot Word to escape commitment. This time the Pivot Word is *likely*.

The key to identifying Pivot Words is this: If a word or group of words appears to allow an author an opening to pivot away from disclosing guilty knowledge or commitment, it may be a Pivot Word

Chapter 5: Pivot Words

EXAMPLES

Draw a small ⯀box⯀ around the word or words when you find Pivot Words in a statement.

Question	Pivot Word (s) in Box
Where were you last night?	I ⯀think⯀ I was at the game.
Did you lock up the house before you left?	I ⯀believe⯀ I locked the front door.
How did he propose to you?	He ⯀kind of⯀ told me he wanted to get married.
Were you at the party when the police arrived?	I ⯀guess⯀ I was at my mom's house when that whole party thing went down.
What did you do at the mall?	We just ⯀sort of⯀ hung out.
What time did you leave work?	⯀Maybe⯀ I left work during the afternoon hours.
How was the weather during the game?	It was ⯀like⯀ raining.
Did you sign up for the contest?	I ⯀may⯀ have.
What time did she leave for college?	It was ⯀somewhat⯀ in the morning when I noticed she wasn't home.
Where did you park the car?	The car was parked ⯀somewhere⯀ near the stadium.
What did you do when you got there?	I walked up to the house, opened the door, and that's ⯀about⯀ it.
Did you do anything along the way?	We ⯀possibly⯀ stopped for a bagel.
Why did you miss the graduation?	I ⯀probably⯀ got into an accident.
What time did your bike get stolen?	As ⯀best as I can recall⯀ it was ⯀around⯀ noon.
I love you. Do you love me?	I ⯀think⯀ I love you too!

PRACTICE EXERCISES

EXERCISE 1

A mother asks her son about a broken lamp. **Draw a box around any Pivot Words** in the son's answers.

> **MOM**: "Did you break the lamp?"
> **SON**: "I don't think so. I was lifting weights in the basement and I think possibly the vibrations from the weights caused it to fall over."
> **MOM**: "Do you expect me to believe the weights did it? The weights are located in a separate room about 30 feet away, and the weights looked like they haven't been touched since I used them yesterday. Why are you lying to me?"
> **SON**: "I'm not lying. I never said it was definitely the weights! I said it was possibly the weights, so it could have been something else. Maybe it was the cat."
> **MOM**: "The cat is outside. Why are you continuing to lie to me?"
> **SON**: "But I'm not lying. I said maybe it was the cat. Oh yeah, now I remember what happened."
> **MOM**: "And?"
> **SON**: "Maybe I accidentally hit the lamp while jumping rope."
> **MOM**: "Maybe?"
> **SON**: "Okay, okay, I did it, but not on purpose."

Answer:

> **MOM**: "Did you break the lamp?"
> **SON**: "I don't think so. I was lifting weights in the basement and possibly the vibrations from the weights caused it to fall over."
> **MOM**: "Do you expect me to believe the weights did it? The weights are located in a separate room about 30 feet away, and the weights looked like they haven't been touched since I used them yesterday. Why are you lying to me?"
> **SON**: "I'm not lying. I never said it was definitely the weights! I said it was possibly the weights, so it could have been something else. Maybe it was the cat."
> **MOM**: "The cat is outside. Why are you continuing to lie to me?"
> **SON**: "But I'm not lying. I said maybe it was the cat. Oh yeah, now I remember what happened."
> **MOM**: "And?"
> **SON**: "Maybe I accidentally hit the lamp while jumping rope."
> **MOM**: "Maybe?"
> **SON**: "Okay, okay, I did it, but not on purpose."

Explanation: The son initially avoids committing to an answer by using the Pivot Words *I don't think so*, *possibly*, and *maybe*. But, his mother also notices he uses these words and questions him until he admits what happened.

EXERCISE 2

A wrestling coach slaps a young man after he lost a match. The young man tells his mother who contacts his school's principal. The principal talks to the coach. **Draw a box around any Pivot Words** you find in the coach's responses.

> PRINCIPAL: "Hey Coach, can we talk?"
> COACH: "Sure, what's up?"
> PRINCIPAL: "Does Ricky Fullnelson wrestle on your team?"
> COACH: "He wrestles at 165 pounds. What's this about?"
> PRINCIPAL: "Did you slap him after he lost his last match?"
> COACH: "I don't believe so."
> PRINCIPAL: "He said you did it in the locker room."
> COACH: "I'm telling you I don't remember doing it!"
> PRINCIPAL: "I saw a video of you doing it. Why are you not telling me the truth?"
> COACH: "I'm not lying. I never said I didn't do it! But now that you mention the video, I do remember a little scuffle involving a slap."

Answer:

> PRINCIPAL: "Hey Coach, can we talk?"
> COACH: "Sure, what's up?"
> PRINCIPAL: "Does Ricky Fullnelson wrestle on your team?"
> COACH: "He wrestles at 165 pounds. What's this about?"
> PRINCIPAL: "Did you slap him after he lost his last match?"
> COACH: "⬚I don't believe so.⬚"
> PRINCIPAL: "He said you did it in the locker room."
> COACH: "I'm telling you ⬚I don't remember⬚ doing it!"
> PRINCIPAL: "I saw a video of you doing it. Why are you not telling me the truth?"
> COACH: "I'm not lying. I never said I didn't do it! But now that you mention the video, I do remember a little scuffle involving a slap."

Explanation: The coach tries not to reveal his guilty knowledge by using the phrases *I don't believe so* and *I don't remember* as linguistic pivots to avoid commitment–until the principal introduces the video.

EXERCISE 3

A man who says he was robbed gives this statement. **Draw a box around any Pivot Words**.

> "I thought I heard two people talking outside my apartment sometime around midnight. I got out of bed to see out of my window. I'm pretty sure I saw two guys standing by the swing set. I think I yelled something at them to make them leave. The next thing I know I'm pretty sure they got me to the ground and I believe they said they were going to like light me up. I guess I passed out at that point. I think I woke up in my living room a few hours later. They took my wallet."

Answer:

> "I [thought] I heard two people talking outside my apartment [sometime] [around] midnight. I got out of bed to see out of my window. I'm [pretty sure] I saw two guys standing by the swing set. I [think] I yelled [something] at them to make them leave. The next thing I know I'm [pretty sure] they got me to the ground and I [believe] they said they were going to [like] light me up. I [guess] I passed out at that point. I [think] I woke up in my living room a [few] hours later. They took my wallet."

Explanation: The man uses 12 Pivot Words or phrases in his statement. Why? Perhaps he has created a false statement to avoid explaining what really happened to his wallet. To find out if he did in fact create a fictional statement, investigators should re-interview him with an emphasis on determining why he uses so many Pivot Words.

EXERCISE 4

The following conversation involves a cab driver and her dispatcher. **Draw a box around the Pivot Words** in the driver's responses.

> CAB DRIVER: "Cab Two to dispatch."
> DISPATCHER: "Go ahead, Cab Two."
> CAB DRIVER: "Can you send a supervisor to my location?"
> SUPERVISOR: "What's the problem?"
> CAB DRIVER: "I was driving south on Wilkerson when I think something ran me off the road."
> SUPERVISOR: "You think something ran you off the road?"
> CAB DRIVER: "I'm pretty sure."

Answer:

> CAB DRIVER: "Cab Two to dispatch."
> DISPATCHER: "Go ahead, Cab Two."
> CAB DRIVER: "Can you send a supervisor to my location?"
> SUPERVISOR: "What's the problem?"
> CAB DRIVER: "I was driving south on Wilkerson when I ⬚think something⬚ ran me off the road."
> SUPERVISOR: "You think something ran you off the road?"
> CAB DRIVER: "I'm ⬚pretty sure.⬚"

Explanation: In this interaction the driver seems to use the phrases *think something* and *pretty sure* to avoid commitment regarding the cause of the accident. To clear up any doubt, the supervisor should ask more questions to determine the reason behind the Pivot Words.

EXERCISE 5

A father asks his son why he came home late last night. **Draw a box around any Pivot Words** in the reply.

> **FATHER**: "Why did you get home so late last night?"
> **SON**: "I know, I know, I know. I was at the basketball game with Jim and Kyle last night. After the game we somehow ended up at the Pyrple Pyzza Planet. We had a pizza and soda. After that we likely walked around a bit and I guess we lost track of time. The next thing I knew it was midnight. As soon as I realized the time, I ran home as fast as I could. That's it."

Answer:

> **FATHER**: "Why did you get home so late last night?"
> **SON**: "I know, I know, I know. I was at the basketball game with Jim and Kyle last night. After the game we ⬚somehow⬚ ended up at the Pyrple Pyzza Planet. We had a pizza and soda. After that we ⬚likely⬚ walked around ⬚a bit⬚ and I ⬚guess⬚ we lost track of time. The next thing I knew it was midnight. As soon as I realized the time, I ran home as fast as I could. That's it."

Explanation: The son uses Pivot Words perhaps to avoid commitment to what he did immediately after he left Pyrple Pyzza Planet. Note: The phrase *next thing I knew* is not a Pivot Word. It is Gap Cover Words discussed in Chapter 9.

EXERCISE 6

A reporter interviews a politician accused of embezzlement. **Draw a box around any Pivot Words**.

> REPORTER: "Is it true you embezzled public funds while in office?"
> POLITICIAN: "I would never steal."
> REPORTER: "Thanks, but that does not answer my question. Did you embezzle public funds while in office?"
> POLITICIAN: "I'm telling you I have plenty of money, so why would I embezzle?"
> REPORTER: "Again, sir, you are not answering my question. Did you embezzle public funds while in office?"
> POLITICIAN: "I don't believe so!"

Answer:

> REPORTER: "Is it true you embezzled public funds while in office?"
> POLITICIAN: "I would never steal."
> REPORTER: "Thanks, but that does not answer my question. Did you embezzle public funds while in office?"
> POLITICIAN: "I'm telling you I have plenty of money, so why would I embezzle?"
> REPORTER: "Again, sir, you are not answering my question. Did you embezzle public funds while in office?"
> POLITICIAN: "\boxed{I don't believe so!}"

Explanation: In this example the politician uses the Pivot Words *I don't believe so* in his final response. The politician could have simply said, *"No"* or *"No I didn't."* He was given the opportunity to do that, but he didn't use it. The interviewer should consider the possibility that the politician uses the Pivot Words *I don't believe so* to avoid commitment to his answer to the question asked.

EXERCISE 7

The following is a statement of a person accused of road rage. **Draw a box around any Pivot Words** in the statement.

> "I was driving home on Route 10 headed to Millston. It was a beautiful day and I didn't have a worry in the world. I was just listening to some music and enjoying myself. That part of the state is really beautiful and has plenty of farms with big pastures. In fact, it reminded me of the trips I made to my cousins' house when I was a kid. The speed limit was 45 and I couldn't have been traveling more than 40 per hour. When I drove by Farmer's Auction House, I noticed a car pull up behind me kind of fast and it was like a foot off my bumper. When the car drove around me there was a lady behind the wheel and I'm pretty sure she flipped me off. The next thing I knew her car sort of collided into mine. We then pulled over and she claimed that I ran her off the road."

Answer:

> "I was driving home on Route 10 headed to Millston. It was a beautiful day and I didn't have a worry in the world. I was just listening to some music and enjoying myself. That part of the state is really beautiful and has plenty of farms with big pastures. In fact, it reminded me of the trips I made to my cousins' house when I was a kid. The speed limit was 45 and I couldn't have been traveling more than 40 per hour. When I drove by Farmer's Auction House, I noticed a car pull up behind me [kind of] fast and it was [like] a foot off my bumper. When the car drove around me there was a lady behind the wheel and I'm [pretty sure] she flipped me off. The next thing I knew her car [sort of] collided into mine. We then pulled over and she claimed that I ran her off the road."

Explanation: In this example the suspect uses the Pivot Words, *kind of*, *like*, *pretty sure*, and *sort of* possibly to avoid commitment to his statement. Did you find it interesting that the suspect doesn't use any Pivot Words until he reaches the Occurrence of Significance?

TIPS

TIP 1 **OTHER REFERENCES TO PIVOT WORDS**

Pivot words can sometimes be referred to as equivocators, qualifiers, or hedges.

TIP 2 **ARE THEY PIVOT WORDS?**

Some statements do not contain Pivot Words. If you are not sure if the word or words you have identified in a statement are Pivot Words, try asking this question: Does the word or group of words used by the author allow the author to avoid commitment to the statement? If so, then consider the possibility that you have identified a Pivot Word or Words.

TIP 3 **BE CAREFUL WHEN FINDING PIVOT WORDS**

If someone provides a statement with Pivot Words, that does not mean that they are definitely trying to avoid commitment or exposure of guilty knowledge. Some people genuinely may not be able to recall an incident and they may need the assistance of Pivot Words to complete their statement. Also, for some people Pivot Words are words used habitually and may be considered an authentic part of their communication baseline.

TIP 4 **LOCATION OF PIVOT WORDS IS IMPORTANT**

Pivot words can be found anywhere in a statement, but I typically would not expect to find them in or around the Occurrence of Significance in a truthful statement. That is where I would expect to find words or phrases that reflect commitment to the statement.

COMPREHENSIVE EXERCISE 2

This exercise reviews all of the previous methodologies. The statement is from a police interview with a woman who says she was the victim of a home invasion.

> "I had just eaten dinner at the Dr. John's Midnite Café located about a quarter-mile south of Peanut's Chat & Chew. It's the place with the blue neon lights and lime green roof. As I was driving, I listened to 96.7 on the radio, the station that plays 70s music 24/7. It took me about 15 minutes to get home. I pulled into the driveway, opened the garage door, turned off the radio, got out, and locked the door. I walked into the garage and as I reached to push the button to close the door, I felt something cover my mouth. I think the person said something. It sounded like a man's voice, so it was probably a man. I guess I fought back and then I likely passed out because I woke up on the floor and the man was now gone. After that I called the police for help."

Steps

1. Draw a [box around] the Occurrence of Significance.
    Calculate the proportion of the Occurrence of Significance here:

2. <u>Underline</u> any High-Quality Sensory Details.

3. <u>Underline</u> any High-Quality Locational Details.

4. Draw a [box] around any Pivot Words.

(Turn page for answers.)

ANSWERS

Occurrence of Significance

> "I had just eaten dinner at the Dr. John's Midnite Café located about a quarter-mile south of Peanut's Chat & Chew. It's the place with the blue neon lights and lime green roof. As I was driving, I listened to 96.7 on the radio, the station that plays 70s music 24/7. It took me about 15 minutes to get home. I pulled into the driveway, opened the garage door, turned off the radio, got out, and locked the door. I walked into the garage and as I reached to push the button to close the door, I felt something cover my mouth. I think the person said something. It sounded like a man's voice, so it was probably a man. I guess I fought back and then I likely passed out because I woke up on the floor and the man was now gone. After that I called the police for help."

Explanation: The Occurrence of Significance starts when the victim describes someone covering her mouth and ends when she says the man was gone. It makes up about 31 percent of the entire statement, meaning that a majority of the victim's statement is dedicated to something other than the Occurrence of Significance. What do you think that indicates?

High-Quality Sensory Details

> "I had just eaten dinner at the Dr. John's Midnite Café located about a quarter-mile south of Peanut's Chat & Chew. It's the place with the blue neon lights and lime green roof. As I was driving, I listened to 96.7 on the radio, the station that plays 70s music 24/7. It took me about 15 minutes to get home. I pulled into the driveway, opened the garage door, turned off the radio, got out, and locked the door. I walked into the garage and as I reached to push the button to close the door, I felt something cover my mouth. I think the person said something. It sounded like a man's voice, so it was probably a man. I guess I fought back and then I likely passed out because I woke up on the floor and the man was now gone. After that I called the police for help."

Explanation: The description of the café's roof and the description of the radio station could be considered High-Quality Sensory Details. These details are good indicators of her commitment to that specific part of the statement. Would you have preferred to see these High-Quality Sensory Details in another part of the statement?

High-Quality Locational Details

> "I had just eaten dinner at the Dr. John's Midnite Café located about a quarter-mile south of Peanut's Chat & Chew. It's the place with the blue neon lights and lime green roof. As I was driving, I listened to 96.7 on the radio, the station that plays 70s music 24/7. It took me about 15 minutes to get home. I pulled into the driveway, opened the garage door, turned off the radio, got out, and locked the door. I walked into the garage and as I reached to push the button to close the door, I felt something cover my mouth. I think the person said something. It sounded like a man's voice, so it was probably a man. I guess I fought back and then I likely passed out because I woke up on the floor and the man was now gone. After that I called the police for help."

Explanation: The victim gives only one High-Quality Locational Detail and it is where she describes the location of the café. The use of this detail is a good indicator of her commitment to that part of the statement. Would you have preferred to see the High-Quality Locational Detail in another part of the statement?

Pivot Words

> "I had just eaten dinner at the Dr. John's Midnite Café located [about] a quarter-mile south of Peanut's Chat & Chew. It's the place with the blue neon lights and lime green roof. As I was driving, I listened to 96.7 on the radio, the station that plays 70s music 24/7. It took me [about] 15 minutes to get home. I pulled into the driveway, opened the garage door, turned off the radio, got out, and locked the door. I walked into the garage and as I reached to push the button to close the door, I felt [something] cover my mouth. I [think] the person said [something]. It sounded [like] a man's voice, so it was [probably] a man. I [guess] I fought back and then I [likely] passed out because I woke up on the floor and the man was now gone. After that I called the police for help."

Explanation: The Pivot Word, *about*, used twice in the beginning of the statement, is not significant because the word is often used habitually to describe distance and time. The victim may be using the remaining Pivot Words to avoid commitment to her statement. The interviewer should consider the possibility that the incident didn't happen or that she is hiding information.

SUMMARY

Did you find it interesting that the author fails to give High-Quality Details in or around the statement's Occurrence of Significance, but instead uses many Pivot Words? What do you think that says about the author's commitment to her statement? Could she have been attempting to avoid exposing guilty knowledge? To answer these questions, the interviewer should re-question the author to determine why she used an abundance of Pivot Words around the Occurrence of Significance.

CHAPTER 6: IRRELEVANT INFORMATION

This chapter examines Irrelevant Information and answers these questions:
- What is Irrelevant Information and how is it recognized in a statement?
- Why would someone provide Irrelevant Information in their statement?
- What does an author's Irrelevant Information tell us about commitment to their statement?

Irrelevant Information is any information that has little or no relevance to the topic or question asked. For example, assume a man says he was attacked in his driveway and a police officer asks him, "What happened?" The man responds, "I woke up and the first thing I did was help my roommate rescue her cat from a tree. I then drove to the blood blank. After donating blood, I walked back to my car and drove home. When I pulled into my driveway and got out of my car, I was attacked. The man punched me repeatedly and when I fought back, he ran away."

In this example, the information about rescuing the cat and donating blood is irrelevant to the conversation because it does not relate to the inquiry. Had the police officer said, "Tell me what happened from the time you woke up until the time you got attacked," this response would have been relevant.

Someone hiding guilty knowledge may give Irrelevant Information to avoid answering the question, to create a favorable perception about themselves for the interviewer, or to explain *why* something happened instead of *what* happened.

> *"Experience has shown ... that a vast, perhaps the larger, portion of the truth arises from the seemingly irrelevant."*
>
> *– Edgar Allan Poe*

TO AVOID ANSWERING THE QUESTION

Some people who want to hide guilty information may avoid answering a question by giving an abundance of Irrelevant Information. Perhaps the hope is to create the impression that they are answering the question, when in fact they are not.

This is similar to a strategy sometimes used by a student whose guilty knowledge is that they don't have an answer to an essay question. That student may hope that writing a long, but irrelevant, answer will create the impression for the teacher that the student has responded to the question. A long, irrelevant response does not equal a quality answer.

TO CREATE A FAVORABLE IMPRESSION

Sometimes people who want to hide guilty information will attempt to give information that creates a favorable perception of their character. Rather than answering the interviewer's question they will amplify such quality traits as honesty, loyalty, or charity. Some interviewers may assume that these traits are exhibited only by truthful people and that the statement must therefore be true. The statement at the start of this chapter–in which the man claimed he had been attacked but provided information about saving a cat and donating blood–is a good example of this.

TO EXPLAIN *WHY*, NOT *WHAT*

Someone who is asked to explain what happened after a significant occurrence will usually describe *what* happened. However, someone who is trying to hide guilty knowledge may explain WHY something happened rather than WHAT happened. Why would someone do this? One reason is that some people who provide false statements fear they will not be believed and that their lie will be exposed. To avoid this exposure a person may find it easier to explain why something happened because that requires less commitment and reduces the possibility of their lie being exposed. However, when someone explains WHY something happened rather than WHAT happened they also increase the likelihood that they have not answered the question, that their answer will be considered irrelevant, or that their irrelevant answer will be noted by the statement examiner.

EXAMPLES

Show Irrelevant Information by ~~marking through~~ the irrelevant words.

When an interviewer asks a victim if they had been hit during a mugging, the interviewer should expect the victim to give a response such as, "Yes, over my left eye" or "No, I wasn't." These answers are acceptable because they are relevant to the question asked and fall within the topic of the conversation. But maybe the mugging victim answers instead:

> "~~I was surprised at how fast you guys got here. I'm good friends with a police dispatcher and he told me you guys were always overworked on Friday nights, so I didn't expect you guys to get here as soon as you did. I don't scare easily but the man who mugged me certainly scared me.~~"

This response is irrelevant to the question and may be a strategy to avoid committing to the statement and to avoid exposing guilty information. The interviewer might wonder: Did the mugging actually occur?

Question	Irrelevant Information
Where were you last night?	~~I got home early.~~
Did you do the laundry?	~~I walked the dog.~~
How did he propose to you?	~~We are planning a small wedding~~
Did you see the robber?	~~Did you know that you are more likely to get robbed when you are alone?~~
What did you do at the museum?	~~I didn't know the museum had over 100 exhibits.~~
What time did you get to work?	~~I always get to work on time.~~
How was the weather during your trip?	~~I love watching football in the fall.~~
Did you sign up for the talent show?	~~I really like competing.~~
How did she get to college?	~~She missed freshman orientation.~~
Where did you park the car?	~~I hate parallel parking.~~
Do you know who stole your money?	~~I found my wallet in the woods.~~
What did you see when you got to the apartment?	~~It took me an hour to get there.~~
Did you make it to the comedy club?	~~I hate driving in the snow.~~
Why did you miss Jerry's birthday?	~~I'll never forget my graduation.~~
Did you meet anyone?	~~I hate work-related parties.~~
What time was your appointment?	~~I will never buy another bike!~~
Did you see the election results?	~~The candidates are lousy.~~

PRACTICE EXERCISES
TO AVOID THE QUESTION

EXERCISE 1

An athlete gives the following statement when a reporter asks him, "Have you ever used performance-enhancing drugs during your career?" **Mark through any Irrelevant Information**.

> "Do you actually think I would do that? I thought you knew better! I've been around that stuff and I know a lot of people who have used that stuff and they claim it helped them. Look, as an athlete I have always taken care of myself and that means keeping a careful eye on everything, and I mean everything that goes into my body. I know a lot of people out there think that because I have broken most records and I continue to play at a very high level for a person of my age, I must be doing something illegal with my body. I think those people are just jealous of me and have no I idea of how hard I work to stay in shape. I mean I have to work at it every day throughout the year. What that means is I am constantly lifting, running, and eating what's right. Do you really think I need performance enhancing drugs? C'mon man, I'm not a cheater!"

Answer:

His entire statement is irrelevant and you should have marked through all of it. Does the athlete respond to the question? Yes. Does he respond with relevancy? No! The question was a simple one that could have been answered with a simple yes or no. But he does not do that. He avoids the question by cramming in 170 words that don't answer the question with relevancy. In this case the athlete may have provided an abundance of Irrelevant Information to create the appearance of being responsive to the question.

Chapter 6: Irrelevant Information 71

EXERCISE 2

A nurse asks a woman how she broke her nose. **Mark through any Irrelevant Information** in the woman's answer.

> **NURSE**: "How did you break your nose?"
> **WOMAN**: "Oh, I don't know. You see my husband and I have been married for 28 years and we have never had a problem. We have three great kids and a beautiful house that we have lived in our entire marriage. I still remember how happy we were when we bought it 25 years ago. We used to take yoga classes together, but now we kind of hang out at the house together feeding the birds and stuff like that. Who would've thought it would have lasted 28 years? Lately, I have had balance issues. I probably fell over the furniture that I must have moved earlier while cleaning the floors. That's basically it."

Answer:

> **NURSE**: "How did you break your nose?"
> **WOMAN**: "Oh, I don't know. ~~You see my husband and I have been married for 28 years and we have never had a problem. We have three great kids and a beautiful house that we have lived in our entire marriage. I still remember how happy we were when we bought it 25 years ago. We used to take yoga classes together, but now we kind of hang out at the house together feeding the birds and stuff like that. Who would've thought it would have lasted 28 years? Lately, I have had balance issues.~~ I probably fell over the furniture that I must have moved earlier while cleaning the floors. That's basically it."

Explanation: Did the woman answer the question with relevancy? Yes, but just barely. Through most of her statement she avoids answering the nurse's question by providing information about her marriage, her kids, her house, her activities with her husband, and her balance issues. It is not until the very end of her response that she finally provides an answer to the question the nurse asked. Did her statement make you curious? Could she have used the Irrelevant Information as a strategy to avoid exposing guilty knowledge? Could something else have happened?

Also, did you notice any Pivot Words? If so, what does that mean to you?

EXERCISE 3

This conversation involves a customer and a car salesman. **Mark through any Irrelevant Information**.

> SALESMAN: "Can I answer any questions for you?"
> CUSTOMER: "I have just one question. What mpg does the MCB-I get?"
> SALESMAN: "Allow me to introduce you to the MCB-II. Do you have children and like to go on vacations?"
> CUSTOMER: "Yes, but I really want the mpg numbers of the MCB-I."
> SALESMAN: "Take a look at the trunk space on the MCB-II. You won't find that on the MCB-I, and you'll need it if you go on vacation to the beach. Think about the chairs, cooler, luggage, umbrella and toys. Where will you put all of that? Not in an MCB-I, I can tell you that!"
> CUSTOMER: "Thanks, but I really want the MCB-I mpg numbers."
> SALESMAN: "Let me show you the interior of the MCB-II. Will you look at that? That is leather my friend. You won't find that in the MCB-I, and you will love that cool leather as you travel to the beach on those hot summer days."
> CUSTOMER: "I just want the numbers."
> SALESMAN: "Okay, it gets 29 mpg."

Answer:

> **SALESMAN**: "Can I answer any questions for you?"
> **CUSTOMER**: "I have just one question. What mpg does the MCB-I get?"
> **SALESMAN**: "~~Allow me to introduce you to the MCB II. Do you have children and like to go on vacations?~~"
> **CUSTOMER**: "Yes, but I really want the mpg numbers of the MCB-I."
> **SALESMAN**: "~~Take a look at the trunk space on the MCB II. You won't find that on the MCB I, and you'll need it if you go on vacation to the beach. Think about the chairs, cooler, luggage, umbrella and toys. Where will you put all of that? Not in an MCB I, I can tell you that!~~"
> **CUSTOMER**: "Thanks, but I really want the MCB-I mpg numbers."
> **SALESMAN**: "~~Let me show you the interior of the MCB II. Will you look at that? That is leather my friend. You won't find that in the MCB I, and you will love that cool leather as you travel to the beach on those hot summer days.~~"
> **CUSTOMER**: "I just want the numbers."
> **SALESMAN**: "Okay, it gets 29 mpg."

Explanation: Did the salesman answer the customer's question with relevancy? Eventually. During most of the conversation the salesman avoids answering by giving information about the MCB-II's storage space and interior. It's not until the end that he finally answers. Why do you think the he didn't immediately provide a relevant response to the question? Did he have something to gain by selling the MCB-II?

TO CREATE A FAVORABLE PERCEPTION

EXERCISE 4

A job interviewer asks a young man why he left his previous job. **Mark through any Irrelevant Information** and think about how the young man uses that information to create a perception.

> "I had been working over 50 hours per week at the warehouse all summer and was preparing to start graduate school on a scholarship in the fall. During my shift I work very hard because I spend most of it lifting heavy boxes and other things. As a result, I get hungry, so on my way to the warehouse I stopped at a convenience store for a sandwich and soda. After leaving the store, I thought about my mom's upcoming birthday and stopped at a drug store and bought her a birthday card. When I got to the warehouse the manager told me I was late and had to let me go. I told him why I was late but he didn't listen to me."

Answer:

> "~~I had been working over 50 hours per week at the warehouse all summer and was preparing to start graduate school on a scholarship in the fall. During my shift I work very hard because I spend most of it lifting heavy boxes and other things. As a result, I get hungry, so on my way to the warehouse I stopped at a convenience store for a sandwich and soda. After leaving the store, I thought about my mom's upcoming birthday and stopped at a drug store and bought her a birthday card.~~ When I got to the warehouse the manager told me I was late and had to let me go. I told him why I was late but he didn't listen to me."

Explanation: The applicant eventually says what caused him to leave his prior job, but only after he provides Irrelevant Information about his work ethics, education, and thoughtfulness–qualities most people would admire. Recall that the interviewer asked him to explain why he lost his previous job, not what makes him a good person. His response does not answer the question he was asked. In this case the interviewer should consider the possibility that the author intentionally provided Irrelevant Information to focus more attention on his admirable traits and less attention on the reason he was released from his job.

EXERCISE 5

Patty is a college junior and is interested in Kenny, a senior, who is in her study group. At the end of the semester, she texts Kenny asking if he is in a relationship. **Mark through any Irrelevant Information** in his response.

> "I can't believe this is my final class of undergraduate work. I'm not sure if you or the study group is aware, but I'm headed to graduate school in the fall. My grades and exam scores are off the charts, so I shouldn't have any problem getting into the aeronautical engineering school at either Tech or State. Apparently those two schools have one the highest job placement records in the country – two years from now I should be in good shape. Who knows, one day I could be an astronaut and lead an expedition to Venus. I know you are also intending to go to grad school in a couple years. Let me know if you want some advice on that. I would be happy to get together to discuss. I'm free on Friday evening."

Answer:

Kenny's entire response is Irrelevant Information and you should have marked through all of it. Did Patty get a response to her question? Yes, but not a relevant one. Kenny responds with 135 words and never answers the question about his relationship status. He tries to create a positive perception of himself by mentioning his educational achievements, his graduate-school plans, and his interest in becoming an aeronautical engineer–attributes that could be appealing to Patty and cause her to ignore the fact that he never answers her question. Patty needs to send him another text explaining that she wants an answer to her question. Good luck Patty!

Exercise 6

Greg and Jackie decide to put a new roof on their house and ask a roofing installer, Paul, to give them an estimate. During the estimate process Jackie asks Paul if his company is insured. **Mark through any Irrelevant Information** in his response. Remember, Jackie asks if his company is insured.

> "We do the job right and we do it fast because we know how important a new roof is to you. I personally train my workers to be careful and to be quick. That's what saves you money and makes us the cheapest company in the business. We don't cut corners we cut prices. In fact, they are so fast at what they do, if we signed a contract today, we could most likely get your new roof done next Wednesday, just five days from now! I don't know if you're getting estimates from anybody else, but I bet no one you talk to can get it done as fast as Fast Boyz Roofs."

Answer:

Paul's entire response is Irrelevant Information and you should have marked through all of it. Did Jackie learn if Paul's company is insured? No. What she learns is that Fast Boyz completes its work fast and that working fast saves money. Paul uses Irrelevant Information possibly to avoid the question and to create the perception in Jackie's mind that Fast Boyz could save her money. If Jackie isn't careful, she may be distracted by Paul's response and forget that he never answers her question. Jackie should ask Paul to answer her question.

Chapter 6: Irrelevant Information

TO EXPLAIN *WHY*, NOT *WHAT*

EXERCISE 7

A woman says her purse was stolen from her car after she parked it outside of a store. A detective asks her what happened. **Mark through the Irrelevant Information** and **determine whether she explains *what* happened or *why* it happened**.

> "It all started when our neighbor's chainsaw gave me a headache. I didn't have any pain reliever and I had to drive to the local drug store and buy some. I used my dad's convertible instead of my car because it was a nice day and I thought having the top down would help my headache. Instead, my headache got worse. I eventually made it to the drug store. My head was really hurting, so I just parked my car and ran in as fast as I could to get some aspirin. In my hurry I guess I left my purse on the front seat of the car and when I went to retrieve it, it was gone. None of this would have happened if it wasn't for my neighbor's chainsaw!"

Answer:

> "~~It all started when our neighbor's chainsaw gave me a headache. I didn't have any pain reliever and I had to drive to the local drug store and buy some. I used my dad's convertible instead of my car because it was a nice day and I thought having the top down would help my headache. Instead, my headache got worse. I eventually made it to the drug store. My head was really hurting,~~ so I just parked my car and ran in as fast as I could to get some aspirin. In my hurry I guess I left my purse on the front seat of the car and when I went to retrieve it, it was gone. ~~None of this would have happened if it wasn't for my neighbor's chainsaw!~~"

Explanation: The detective asks the victim what happened when her purse was stolen. She uses most of her statement to explain *why*. She says her purse was stolen because she heard her neighbor's chainsaw and that gave her a headache, so she drove her father's convertible to the store to get medicine. While driving her headache worsened causing her to leave her purse in the car. Finally her purse was stolen from the car.

She could have simply said, as she eventually does, that she left her purse in the car and when she returned the purse was gone. The interviewers may consider that something else happened to the victim's purse, something that she may have been too embarrassed or ashamed to report.

EXERCISE 8

A man tells his insurance company that he was carjacked when driving home from work. **Mark through the Irrelevant Information. Does it explain *what* happened or *why* it happened?**

> "I was driving home from work just minding my own business and listening to some music. As I drove by the Boxer exit, I decided to check out a short cut, so I decided to get off the main road and take old Route 871 for the rest of my ride home. After I got on 871, I drove for about two miles and saw a car broken down on the side of the road and that reminded me that a few weeks ago I heard a noise coming from the front of my car. I decided that now would probably be a good time to take a quick peek under the hood, so I looked for a safe place to check it out and I pulled into the parking lot of Trixie's Ace Motel to check my car's problem. At first, I decided to pull into a parking space located in front of the motel but I decided against that because I didn't want to take the parking space of a customer, you know what I mean? So, as soon as I pulled around back behind a dumpster to privately inspect my car, a man approached. I thought he was there to help me, but he pulled out a gun and told me to get out of my car."

Chapter 6: Irrelevant Information

Answer:

> "~~I was driving home from work just minding my own business and listening to some music. As I drove by the Boxer exit, I decided to check out a short cut, so I decided to get off the main road and take old Route 871 for the rest of my ride home. After I got on 871, I drove for about two miles and saw a car broken down on the side of the road and that reminded me that a few weeks ago I heard a noise coming from the front of my car. I decided that now would probably be a good time to take a quick peek under the hood, so I looked for a safe place to check it out and I pulled into the parking lot of Trixie's Ace Motel to check my car's problem. At first, I decided to pull into a parking space located in front of the motel but I decided against that because I didn't want to take the parking space of a customer, you know what I mean?~~ So, as soon as I pulled around back behind a dumpster to privately inspect my car, a man approached. I thought he was there to help me, but he pulled out a gun and told me to get out of my car."

Explanation: The victim uses most of his statement to explain *why* his vehicle was stolen. He took a short cut home during which he saw a disabled car. He remembered a noise his own car had made so he pulled behind a dumpster in a motel parking lot to check out his car. Finally he was carjacked. Did the victim need to provide so much Irrelevant Information? He could have simply said that he pulled over to inspect his car and was carjacked.

Some people who manipulate their statement may not have confidence in their story, finding it easier to explain *why* something happened rather than *what* happened. This victim may have stuffed his statement with Irrelevant Information to convince the interviewer *why* the carjacking happened instead of *what* happened. Could he have had other motives for being at the motel when his car was taken? Was his car actually stolen?

ALL TYPES OF IRRELEVANT INFORMATION

EXERCISE 9

A factory explodes and an investigator asks an employee to explain what he did from when he arrived at work until he called 911. **Mark through any Irrelevant Information** and **determine its purpose.**

> "I came into work as I usually do. I was running a little late because I stayed up last night watching the baseball game. It was good. It went into extra innings and it finally ended when Jones hit a home run. When I got to work, I punched in as I normally do and worked the binding machine like I normally do. No problem there. I've been working that machine for over 10 years and haven't had an accident yet. In fact, during the last employee's conference, the owner mentioned my work history and gave me a gift certificate for Jax Rib Shack located on Fifth and Arcola. I haven't been there in years and I plan to take my wife. She loves that place, and really likes their pulled pork special. At noon I went to the binding supply room and probably checked on some stuff. I probably left there and checked on a few things – possibly in the storage areas. Just before I left for lunch, I heard a loud explosion. The smoke alarms sounded and I saw a heavy gray cloud of smoke filling the factory. I then told everyone to leave and called 911. I personally saved five people by getting them out of the factory."

What type of Irrelevant Information did you find? _____

Answer:

> "I came into work as I usually do. ~~I was running a little late because I stayed up last night watching the baseball game. It was good. It went into extra innings and it finally ended when Jones hit a home run.~~ When I got to work, I punched in as I normally do and worked the binding machine like I normally do. No problem there. ~~I've been working that machine for over 10 years and haven't had an accident yet. In fact, during the last employee's conference, the owner mentioned my work history and gave me a gift certificate for Jax Rib Shack located on Fifth and Areola. I haven't been there in years and I plan to take my wife. She loves that place, and really likes their pulled pork special.~~ At noon I went to the binding supply room and probably checked on some stuff. I probably left there and checked on a few things – possibly in the storage areas. Just before I left for lunch, I heard a loud explosion. The smoke alarms sounded and I saw a heavy gray cloud of smoke filling the factory. I then told everyone to leave and called 911. ~~I personally saved five people by getting them out of the factory.~~"

Explanation: The employee uses Irrelevant Information near the beginning and in the middle of his statement–possibly to create a perception that he is being responsive and cooperating with the investigation. Specifically, he gives a large amount of Irrelevant Information about a baseball game, his history of safety at work, and Jax Rib Shack. Remember, providing an abundance of information doesn't necessarily mean the person is cooperating. In the last two lines of his statement the employee uses Irrelevant Information to create a positive perception about himself –specifically to imply that he is a hero for saving five lives.

Did you notice his Pivot Words around the time of explosion?

EXERCISE 10

This is an interview with the CEO of Neva's Place, a chain of more than 100 restaurants that recently closed several locations. Sources close to the CEO confided to a journalist that the restaurant chain is in financial distress. During an interview, the reporter asks Neva's CEO, "Is Neva's going to file for bankruptcy?" **Mark through any Irrelevant Information** in the CEO's answer and **determine the type of Irrelevant Information.**

> "Neva's is a sports-themed restaurant chain headquartered in the Southwestern United States. Our first restaurant was opened in 1995. We now have a total of 112 franchises throughout the Western United States. Our biggest fan is baseball player Frank Hurler. He loves our food and endorses it whenever he gets the chance. He is a personal friend and I spoke to him just last week. He told me he was expecting to do well this year and believes he may have a shot at winning the Fast Ball Award. I hope he wins it because he's a great guy and family man. Regarding your question, Neva's is basically in great financial shape."

What type of Irrelevant Information did you find? _____

Answer:

> "~~Neva's is a sports-themed restaurant chain headquartered in the Southwestern United States. Our first restaurant was opened in 1995. We now have a total of 112 franchises throughout the Western United States. Our biggest fan is baseball player Frank Hurler. He loves our food and endorses it whenever he gets the chance. He is a personal friend and I spoke to him just last week. He told me he was expecting to do well this year and believes he may have a shot at winning the Fast Ball Award. I hope he wins it because he's a great guy and family man.~~ Regarding your question, Neva's is basically in great financial shape."

Nearly the entire statement is Irrelevant Information. The CEO initially avoids a direct response to his interviewer's question by front-loading his statement with Irrelevant Information that could create a sense of responsiveness and cooperation and give a favorable impression about Neva's. He avoids answering the question until he reaches his last sentence. Did you notice the Pivot Word he used to finally answer the question? Do you feel comfortable with his response?

EXERCISE 11

This statement is from a factory owner who is selling his company. A potential buyer asks him, "What were the results of your company's most recent government pollution inspection?" **Mark through any Irrelevant Information** and **determine the CEO's intent** in using it.

> "I believe the federal government passed tougher laws regarding the burning of fossil fuels a few years back and my attorneys were supposed to ensure those laws were met but they didn't. We had also hired a new engineer at the time to handle that sort of stuff. He was supposed to be an expert in that area. Well, he wasn't. In fact, I later found out he didn't even have an engineering degree. But he was able to fool my HR into thinking he was the real deal. We failed the inspection and received a fine. If only I had known the inspectors were coming, I could have ensured our scrubbers were working and we could have passed inspection."

What type of Irrelevant Information did you find? _____

Answer:

> "~~I believe the federal government passed tougher laws regarding the burning of fossil fuels a few years back and my attorneys were supposed to ensure those laws were met but they didn't. We had also hired a new engineer at the time to handle that sort of stuff. He was supposed to be an expert in that area. Well, he wasn't. In fact, I later found out he didn't even have an engineering degree. But he was able to fool my HR into thinking he was the real deal.~~ We failed the inspection and received a fine. ~~If only I had known the inspectors were coming, I could have ensured our scrubbers were working and we could have passed inspection.~~"

Explanation: The owner initially avoids a direct response to the potential buyer's question by providing Irrelevant Information that doesn't explain what the results of the inspection were, but rather explains why his company failed the inspection. The original question was about *what* the results of his company's most recent inspection were, not *why* his company failed the inspection.

TIPS

TIP 1   **ASK QUESTIONS TO DETERMINE IRRELEVANT INFORMATION**

If you agree with the following questions, then you likely have identified Irrelevant Information:

- Do you agree, that given the context, the information avoids answering the question with relevancy?
- Do you agree that the statement makes sense when read without the identified irrelevant words?

TIP 2   **IRRELEVANT INFORMATION MAY NOT INDICATE GUILTY KNOWLEDGE**

Not all Irrelevant Information is intended to protect guilty knowledge. Some authors may provide Irrelevant Information because they fear being disbelieved, are insecure, or have a naturally occurring linguistic trait.

TIP 3   **IRRELEVANT INFORMATION CAN BE FOUND ANYWHERE IN A STATEMENT**

TIP 4   **OPINIONS AND INFORMATION IN PARENTHESES MAY BE IRRELEVANT**

When an author provides a personal opinion in their statement it usually falls outside the scope of the conversation and can be considered irrelevant. The same is true for information placed inside parentheses. An example of this is a statement from a man who lost his wedding band:

"I went to the hotel and checked in. I then met a client for a couple of drinks (~~she asked to meet with me to talk about some kind computer issues~~). Before I met her I put my wedding band by the sink in my room. When I returned it was gone. ~~My bet is the cleaning staff took it while I was out. They seem to be sketchy.~~"

The information in parentheses and the opinion he offers at the end fall outside the scope of the relevant conversation.

COMPREHENSIVE EXERCISE 3

This exercise uses the following statement to review the previous methodologies. A detective questions a man who says he was robbed while walking to the bank to make a deposit. The detective asks, "What happened?"

> "I am the manager of Sooky's Arcade and Bar. I closed the bar at 11:00 pm as I always do because I am the night manager. I have been working as the manager at Sooky's for 11 years and nothing like this has ever happened. My uncle and his friends who are with the city police told me to be careful when handling my deposits and I've always remembered that. I am just happy I am okay because my mother counts on me for financial support. She is on disability. It's so hard trying to find a decent job in this area due to the factory closing and all. I can remember how safe it was while growing up and no one ever had a problem then. I guess things are different now. I just hope things get better because this is a great town, with great schools, parks and people. After I was finished closing, I took the night deposit and headed to the bank. I walked down Fifth Street and noticed one of the streetlights was out, making it very dark and very dangerous. As I got near the bank, I thought I heard a noise and when I looked around, I was probably grabbed from behind and pushed to the ground. He told me not to move or he would stab me. I think he grabbed the money. He also took my wallet and my phone. He left. I ran to a convenience store and told all of the people there to call the police because I had been robbed. One lady called the police. I then called my boss and told him what happened and waited for you guys to get here. That's just about it."

Steps

1. Draw a ⬚box around⬚ the Occurrence of Significance.
     Calculate the proportion of the Occurrence of Significance here:

2. <u>Underline</u> any High-Quality Sensory Details.
3. <u>Underline</u> any High-Quality Locational Details.
4. Draw a ⬚box⬚ around any Pivot Words.
5. ~~Mark through~~ any Irrelevant Information.

(Turn page for answers.)

ANSWERS

Occurrence of Significance

> "I am the manager of Sooky's Arcade and Bar. I closed the bar at 11:00 pm as I always do because I am the night manager. I have been working as the manager at Sooky's for 11 years and nothing like this has ever happened. My uncle and his friends who are with the city police told me to be careful when handling my deposits and I've always remembered that. I am just happy I am okay because my mother counts on me for financial support. She is on disability. It's so hard trying to find a decent job in this area due to the factory closing and all. I can remember how safe it was while growing up and no one ever had a problem then. I guess things are different now. I just hope things get better because this is a great town, with great schools, parks and people. After I was finished closing, I took the night deposit and headed to the bank. I walked down Fifth Street and noticed one of the streetlights was out, making it very dark and very dangerous. As I got near the bank, I thought I heard a noise and when I looked around, ⎡I was probably grabbed from behind and pushed to the ground. He told me not to move or he would stab me. I think he grabbed the money. He also took my wallet and my phone. He left.⎦ I ran to a convenience store and told all of the people there to call the police because I had been robbed. One lady called the police. I then called my boss and told him what happened and waited for you guys to get here. That's just about it."

Explanation: The Occurrence of Significance starts when the man says that someone grabbed him and ends when that person leaves. The Occurrence of Significance makes up about 13 percent of the overall statement, indicating that 87 percent of his statement is outside the Occurrence of Significance. These numbers reflect a low level of commitment by the author. Could the author have intentionally compressed the Occurrence of Significance to decrease the possibility of exposing guilty knowledge? Did the robbery actually occur as reported?

Comprehensive Exercise 3 87

High-Quality Sensory Details & High-Quality Locational Details

Explanation: NONE. This statement has many details, but none of them are High-Quality Sensory Details or High Quality Locational Details. Remember, High-Quality Sensory and Locational Details show a high level of commitment. In this statement those details just aren't there.

Pivot Words

> "I am the manager of Sooky's Arcade and Bar. I closed the bar at 11:00 pm as I always do because I am the night manager. I have been working as the manager at Sooky's for 11 years and nothing like this has ever happened. My uncle and his friends who are with the city police told me to be careful when handling my deposits and I've always remembered that. I am just happy I am okay because my mother counts on me for financial support. She is on disability. It's so hard trying to find a decent job in this area due to the factory closing and all. I can remember how safe it was while growing up and no one ever had a problem then. I [guess] things are different now. I just hope things get better because this is a great town, with great schools, parks and people. After I was finished closing, I took the night deposit and headed to the bank. I walked down Fifth Street and noticed one of the streetlights was out, making it very dark and very dangerous. As I got near the bank, I [thought] I heard a noise and when I looked [around], I was [probably] grabbed from behind and pushed to the ground. He told me not to move or he would stab me. I [think] he grabbed the money. He also took my wallet and my phone. He left. I ran to a convenience store and told all of the people there to call the police because I had been robbed. One lady called the police. I then called my boss and told him what happened and waited for you guys to get here. That's [just about it.]"

Explanation: The victim uses six Pivot Words or phrases in his statement, which is concerning because most of the words allow him to avoid being specific about the robbery. Why would he do that?

Irrelevant Information

> "~~I am the manager of Sooky's Arcade and Bar. I closed the bar at 11:00 pm as I always do because I am the night manager. I have been working as the manager at Sooky's for 11 years and nothing like this has ever happened. My uncle and his friends who are with the city police told me to be careful when handling my deposits and I've always remembered that. I am just happy I am okay because my mother counts on me for financial support. She is on disability. It's so hard trying to find a decent job in this area due to the factory closing and all. I can remember how safe it was while growing up and no one ever had a problem then. I~~ guess ~~things are different now. I just hope things get better because this is a great town, with great schools, parks and people~~. After I was finished closing, I took the night deposit and headed to the bank. I walked down Fifth Street and ~~noticed one of the streetlights was out, making it very dark and very dangerous~~. As I got near the bank, I thought I heard a noise and when I looked around, I was probably grabbed from behind and pushed to the ground. He told me not to move or he would stab me. I think he grabbed the money. He also took my wallet and my phone. He left. I ran to a convenience store and told all of the people there to call the police because I had been robbed. One lady called the police. I then called my boss and told him what happened and waited for you guys to get here. That's just about it."

Explanation: The victim dedicates the beginning of his statement to the factory closing, to previously safe conditions of the city, and to the past quality of the parks and schools. This is irrelevant because it avoids the question. It adds to the length of his statement and could create the impression that he is cooperating–something that may be seen as favorable. The victim also explains that he has been the manager of Sooky's Arcade and Bar for 11 years, that his uncle is a police officer, and that he helps to financially support his mother who is on disability.

This information is irrelevant to the question and may be an attempt to create the perception that he is loyal to his job, supports law enforcement, and takes care of his disabled mother.

Finally the victim explains that while he was walking to the bank he noticed one of the streetlights was not working, making his walk dark and dangerous. This information has weak relevance to the detective's question, but in using it he explains why the robbery happened–darkness made the environment perfect for a robbery.

SUMMARY

This robbery victim gives a lot of Irrelevant Information, more than half of his statement. He suggests that he is a person of good character, a person who is cooperating with the robbery investigation, and a person who must have been robbed because he gives a good reason *why* the robbery happened, rather than simply stating *what* happened. In addition, the statement has a small Occurrence of Significance at about 13 percent; it doesn't contain any High-Quality Sensory or Locational Details; and it does contain several Pivot Words in and around the Occurrence of Significance. The detective should be concerned about the victim's statement and consider the possibility it may have been manipulated to hide guilty information.

CHAPTER 7: TIME MARKERS

This chapter discusses Time Markers found in statements. Specifically, it will answer:
- What are Time Markers?
- How do you recognize Time Markers in a statement?
- What do Time Markers tell us about an author's commitment to their statement?

Time Markers are references to time found in a statement. Examining Time Markers helps us compare an author's alleged activities against the time he says they occurred and note any discrepancies. These discrepancies should be explored to determine if the author is trying to avoid exposing guilty knowledge.

Time markers can be direct or indirect. When analyzing a statement, it is important to locate and analyze both.

A direct Time Marker is actual time, such as 3:45 pm, at a quarter to 11 am, and 7:05 am. It is an exact reference to time.

An indirect Time Marker is a general time reference such as: "a couple of hours later" or "around six hours ago." In this case a specific (or direct) time is not provided, but instead a reference to time is.

"No man has a good enough memory to be a successful liar."

—Abraham Lincoln

EXAMPLES

Draw a (circle) around any Time Markers that you find in a statement.

Question	Time Marker
What time did you leave the party?	I left at 3:00 pm. (direct marker)
When did you leave the mall?	I took off at 11:30 am. (direct marker)
What time was the accident?	It happened at 3:05 am. (direct marker)
What time did you get to the store?	Thirty minutes ago. (indirect marker)
When will the pool open?	It opens in a couple of hours. (indirect marker)
When did you get to work?	At a quarter to 7:00. (direct marker)
What time did you go to bed?	At half past 9:00 pm. (direct marker)
How long were you in the house?	About 20 minutes. (indirect marker)
How long were you on break?	Around 40 minutes. (indirect marker)

Example Statement

In this example, a man is accused of being absent from work without clocking out. His employer asks him to explain his morning activities on the day of his suspected absence. This is his statement:

> At 5:30 am I woke up and took a shower and shaved.
> At 5:45 am I got dressed.
> At 6:00 am I walked Sam. Sam is my dog.
> At 6:30 am I returned home and made my lunch.
> At 6:45 am I left for work.
> At 7:00 am I caught the bus.
> At 7:30 am I arrived at work, got some coffee and worked on the Blue Orange account.
> At 9:30 am I went to the office snack machines.
> At 11:30 am I worked on another account.
> At 11:45 am I went to lunch.
> At noon I returned from lunch.

Explanation: The statement has 11 Time Markers. To see how these markers reveal the author's commitment we can break down the employee's statement and compare the activities that the employee itemizes against the times that he says they occurred. For instance, in line 1 the employee says he got up at 5:30 am to shower and shave, then he says he got dressed at 5:45 am. The duration of this activity, showering and shaving, is 15 minutes. In line 3 the employee says he walked his dog at 6:00 am. Subtracting the author's prior time marker of 5:45 am, we can see he spent 15 minutes getting dressed.

Using this procedure for each Time Marker, we can detail the employee's timeline as follows:

- 30 minutes to walk his dog.
- 15 minutes to prepare his lunch.
- 15 minutes to catch the bus.
- 30 minutes to ride the bus ride to work.
- 120 minutes to get coffee and work on an account.
- 120 minutes to visit the vending machines.
- 15 minutes to work on another account.
- 15 minutes for lunch.

In reviewing this breakdown of the employee's reported activities we can see that the time he expends for each of the activities seems reasonable–except for the 120 minutes he spends visiting the vending machines. Why did the employee spend so much time at the vending machines instead of at his desk? Did he do something other than what he says? Could his response be an attempt to avoid exposing guilty information such as leaving work without clocking out? To answer these questions, the employer should re-interview the employee with the intent of determining exactly what he did while visiting the vending machines for two hours.

PRACTICE EXERCISES

EXERCISE 1

This statement is from a woman who says her vehicle was stolen. The interviewer asks her to explain everything that happened from the time she had lunch until she contacted the police. **Circle any direct or indirect Time Markers** and **determine if they cause you concern**.

> "At noon I had lunch at Mountain Man's Restaurant. Then at 1:00 this afternoon I drove my mom's car to PUD's Job Solutions to find a job. It took me a half hour to get there. Once I was there, I was interviewed and they asked me all sorts of questions. I also filled out some forms. After an hour I left PUD's and drove around for an hour. At 3:30 I stopped someplace and filled out an application and stuff like that. I left there at about 7:30 and started home on Route 222 and my mom's car was making a weird sound about 15 minutes into my drive, so I pulled into a parking lot and left to get help. When I returned my mom's car was gone. I then called the police and they told me they found my car crashed on the side of Route 222."

Use this space to write any Time Markers and their associated activity. Do you have any concerns?

Answer:

> "At (noon) I had lunch at Mountain Man's Restaurant. Then at (1:00) this afternoon I drove my mom's car to PUD's Job Solutions to find a job. It took me a (half hour) *(now 1:30)* to get there. Once I was there, I was interviewed and they asked me all sorts of questions. I also filled out some forms. After (an hour) *(now 2:30)* I left PUD's and drove around for (an hour). At (3:30) I stopped someplace and filled out an application and stuff like that. I left there at about (7:30) and started home on Route 222 and my mom's car was making a weird sound (about 15 minutes) *(now 7:45)* into my drive, so I pulled into a parking lot and left to get help. When I returned my mom's car was gone. I then called the police and they told me they found my car crashed on the side of Route 222."

Explanation: While reviewing this statement, I converted indirect Time Markers in the statement into direct Time Markers (shown in parentheses). Doing this helps me to figure out the duration of each activity. In this example there are eight Time Markers that represent six activities. Associating each activity with its Time Markers you should have a timeline that looks like this:

- 60 minutes to eat lunch.
- 30 minutes to drive to PUD's.
- 60 minutes spent at PUD's.
- 60 minutes to drive around.
- 240 minutes to stop someplace and fill out an application.
- 15 minutes to start home before stopping.

The duration of each of the woman's activities seems reasonable and verifiable, except for the 240 minutes she spent *someplace*. Why did she spend so much time *someplace*? Does *someplace* have a name? Did something happen at *someplace* that could have caused her shame or embarrassment? Was it a coincidence that her visit to *someplace* occurred just before the theft of the car? For answers to these questions, the woman should be re-interviewed to determine more about her use of the word *someplace* and why she spent four hours there.

Did you notice any Pivot Words in her statement? If so, do those words mean anything to you?

EXERCISE 2

This case involves a business that discovers $10,000 missing from its safe on a Monday evening. A day later the owner asks an employee who had access to the safe to write a statement about everything he did at work on Monday. **Circle any Time Markers and determine if they cause you concern.**

> "I came into work at 8:00 am like I always do. As soon as I arrived, I made some coffee and talked with some people for about 15 minutes. I then started working at my desk filling out the orders that came in during the weekend. That lasted about 30 minutes and then I went to the bathroom for about 10 minutes. I met some friends outside the bathroom and we chatted for a bit. I got back to my cubicle at 9:10 am and read and responded to some e-mails until 10:30 am. I then went to Mike's office for my performance review and left there at 11:30 am. I went back to my cubicle and started processing more orders. I went to lunch at noon. During lunch I talked to Pat and Diane about last night's basketball game and had some spaghetti. I got back to my cube at 12:30 pm and processed some more orders while I also ate my dessert. I love ice cream sandwiches. At 1:30 pm I did some boring stuff around the office and returned to my cubicle at 3:00 pm. Then I helped out the mailroom guy until 4:00 pm. I then went back to my cube and processed orders and returned emails until I went home at 4:30 pm."

Use this space to write any Time Markers and their associated activity. Do you have any concerns?

Answer:

> "I came into work at **8:00 am** like I always do. As soon as I arrived, I made some coffee and talked with some people for **about 15 minutes** *(now 8:15)*. I then started working at my desk filling out the orders that came in during the weekend. That lasted **about 30 minutes** *(now 8:45)* and then I went to the bathroom for **about 10 minutes** *(now 8:55)*. I met some friends outside the bathroom and we chatted for a bit. I got back to my cubicle at **9:10 am** and read and responded to some e-mails until **10:30 am**. I then went to Mike's office for my performance review and left there at **11:30 am**. I went back to my cubicle and started processing more orders. I went to lunch at **noon**. During lunch I talked to Pat and Diane about last night's basketball game and had some spaghetti. I got back to my cube at **12:30 pm** and processed some more orders while I also ate my dessert. I love ice cream sandwiches. At **1:30 pm** I did some boring stuff around the office and returned to my cubicle at **3:00 pm**. Then I helped out the mailroom guy until **4:00 pm**. I then went back to my cube and processed orders and returned emails until I went home at **4:30 pm**."

Explanation: There are 13 Time Markers representing 12 activities. The timeline of his activities looks like this:

- 15 minutes to make coffee and talk
- 30 minutes to work at desk.
- 10 minutes to use the bathroom.
- 15 minutes to chat with friends.
- 80 minutes to work in cubicle.
- 60 minutes for performance review.
- 30 minutes to process orders.
- 30 minutes for lunch.
- 60 minutes to process orders.
- 90 minutes to do boring stuff.
- 60 minutes to help mailroom guy.
- 30 minutes to process orders.

The activities described by the employee are detailed and appear to be reasonable for the durations of time stated–except for the 90 minutes he spent *doing boring stuff*. What exactly is *boring stuff*? Could he have used the words *boring stuff* to mask something he didn't want exposed? Did the employee steal the money? Possibly. The employee should be re-interviewed to determine exactly what he did during the 90 minutes he spent *doing boring stuff*.

EXERCISE 3

This statement is from a woman suspected of involvement in a burglary at 10:30 pm the previous evening. When questioned about the burglary she says she was visiting her mother at the time and provides a statement about that visit. **Circle any direct or indirect Time Markers and determine if they cause you concern.**

> "I left my house at 6:00 pm. I reached my mom's house at about 6:30 pm. I helped her with cooking the food (we had some salad and chicken teriyaki). I also set the table. We ate about a half-hour after my arrival. When we were finished, around 7:30 pm now, I cleaned up the table, fed the dog, and did the dishes for about a half-hour. Next, I walked the dog around the block for about 15 minutes. We then went to the living room and mom showed me some pictures she had taken from her last cruise to Hawaii. She usually cruises about twice a year and takes lots of photos. After looking at the photos, we watched the end of the football game. It ended in a stupid tie at around 9:00 pm. We then chatted briefly about some things until midnight. I then left and got home at 12:30 am."

Use this space to write any Time Markers and their associated activity. Do you have any concerns?

Answer

> "I left my house at (6:00 pm.) I reached my mom's house (at about 6:30) pm. I helped her with cooking the food (we had some salad and chicken teriyaki). I also set the table. We ate (about a half-hour) after my arrival. When we were finished, (around 7:30 pm) now, I cleaned up the table, fed the dog, and did the dishes for about (a half-hour) *(now 8 pm)*. Next, I walked the dog around the block for about (15 minutes) *(now 8:15 pm)*. We then went to the living room and mom showed me some pictures she had taken from her last cruise to Hawaii. She usually cruises about twice a year and takes lots of photos. After looking at the photos, we watched the end of the football game. It ended in a stupid tie at around (9:00 pm) We then chatted briefly about some things until (midnight) I then left and got home at (12:30 am)."

Explanation: In this example there are nine Time Markers representing eight activities–the woman uses both direct and indirect references to times. This is her timeline:

- 30 minutes to drive to mom's house.
- 30 minutes to help with dinner.
- 30 minutes to eat dinner.
- 30 minutes to clean up and feed the dog.
- 15 minutes to walk the dog.
- 45 minutes to look at photos and watch a football game.
- 180 minutes to chat briefly about some things.
- 30 minutes to drive home.

The time spent for each of her activities seems reasonable–except for the 180 minutes she spent *chatting briefly about some things*. This is concerning because it reflects a lack of commitment and it occurs at the same time as the burglary. What do you suppose they talked about and why do you think it took so long to do it? Could the woman have done something else during those 180 minutes? Armed with this information, the suspect should be re-interviewed to determine exactly what happened during her *brief chat* with her mother.

TIPS

TIP 1   **IT'S NOT UNUSUAL TO FIND PIVOT WORDS WITH TIME MARKERS**

Often, when someone provides a Time Marker it will be preceded by a Pivot Word such as *around* or *about*. Usually, these Pivot Words are not of any concern because many people have a communication baseline that includes providing a Pivot Word prior to a time reference.

Here's an example:
Husband: "What time is it?"
Wife: "It's *about* 2:30"
Husband: "Thanks. Do you know what time Phillip called this morning?"
Wife: "*Around* 9:00 am."

TIP 2   **TIME MARKERS ARE FREQUENTLY ABSENT**

Some statements do not have Time Markers. In fact, many do not. This happens because some people do not provide them in their statements unless specifically asked.

TIP 3   **TRY NOT TO ASK FOR TIME MARKERS**

If possible, try to avoid specifically asking someone to provide specific times or references to time in their statement. Such a request is considered statement framing and may contaminate the statement.

TIP 4   **LOCATION OF TIME MARKERS IS IMPORTANT**

Time Markers in and around the Occurrence of Significance help show commitment to the statement.

COMPREHENSIVE EXERCISE 4

Investigators ask a man who says he was kidnapped at a carwash: "What happened?"

"I left my business at 8:30 pm and went to the Suds & Stuff Car Wash located at the corner of Penn and Wright streets and across from Ponzi's donuts sometime in the evening to clean and wash my car. I just purchased it last month and it is ruby red with gold pin stripes and has a 500 horse power engine. I never race it on the streets because that would be a stupid thing to do. I know people who do that and they get themselves into trouble. It was 9:00 pm and no one else was there probably because, in my opinion, of all the crime that happens there. Next, I started vacuuming the car. I was forced to lay face down on the back floor as my kidnappers drove me. I guess they took my wallet. Later, they had me make numerous withdrawals from my bank account. This probably lasted all night. Next thing you know I'm alone in my car at 5:30 am. I basically found my phone and wallet in the car and called my business partner at 7:30 am and told him I had been kidnapped and most of our money from our business account was taken. He told me to call the police, so I did."

Steps

1. Draw a [box around] the Occurrence of Significance. Calculate the proportion.
2. <u>Underline</u> High-Quality Sensory Details.
3. <u>Underline</u> High-Quality Locational Details.
4. Draw a [box] around any Pivot Words.
5. ~~Mark through~~ any Irrelevant Information.
6. Draw a (circle) around any Time Markers.

(Turn page for answers.)

ANSWERS

Occurrence of Significance

> "I left my business at 8:30 pm and went to the Suds & Stuff Car Wash located at the corner of Penn and Wright streets and across from Ponzi's donuts sometime in the evening to clean and wash my car. I just purchased it last month and it is ruby red with gold pin stripes and has a 500 horse power engine. I never race it on the streets because that would be a stupid thing to do. I know people who do that and they get themselves into trouble. It was 9:00 pm and no one else was there probably because, in my opinion, of all the crime that happens there. Next, I started vacuuming the car. ⌈I was forced to lay face down on the back floor as my kidnappers drove me. I guess they took my wallet. Later, they had me make numerous withdrawals from my bank account. This probably lasted all night. Next thing you know I'm alone in my car at 5:30 am.⌋ I basically found my phone and wallet in the car and called my business partner at 7:30 am and told him I had been kidnapped and most of our money from our business account was taken. He told me to call the police, so I did."

Explanation: The Occurrence of Significance starts when the victim describes being forced to lay on the car floor and ends when he finds himself alone in his car. The Occurrence of Significance is about 22 percent of the statement.

Comprehensive Exercise 4

High-Quality Sensory & Locational Details

> "I left my business at 8:30 pm and went to the Suds & Stuff Car Wash located at the <u>corner of Penn and Wright streets and across from Ponzi's donuts</u> sometime in the evening to clean and wash my car. I just purchased it last month and it is <u>ruby red with gold pin stripes and has a 500 horse power engine</u>. I never race it on the streets because that would be a stupid thing to do. I know people who do that and they get themselves into trouble. It was 9:00 pm and no one else was there probably because, in my opinion, of all the crime that happens there. Next, I started vacuuming the car. I was forced to lay face down on the back floor as my kidnappers drove me. I guess they took my wallet. Later, they had me make numerous withdrawals from my bank account. This probably lasted all night. Next thing you know I'm alone in my car at 5:30 am. I basically found my phone and wallet in the car and called my business partner at 7:30 am and told him I had been kidnapped and most of our money from our business account was taken. He told me to call the police, so I did."

Explanation: The description of his car is consistent with authorial commitment to that portion of the statement, as is the locational reference for the car wash. Did you find any of these details in or around the statement's Occurrence of Significance?

Pivot Words

> "I left my business at 8:30 pm and went to the Suds & Stuff Car Wash located at the corner of Penn and Wright streets and across from Ponzi's donuts sometime in the evening to clean and wash my car. I just purchased it last month and it is ruby red with gold pin stripes and has a 500 horse power engine. I never race it on the streets because that would be a stupid thing to do. I know people who do that and they get themselves into trouble. It was 9:00 pm and no one else was there probably because, in my opinion, of all the crime that happens there. Next, I started vacuuming the car. I was forced to lay face down on the back floor as my kidnappers drove me. I guess they took my wallet. Later, they had me make numerous withdrawals from my bank account. This probably lasted all night. Next thing you know I'm alone in my car at 5:30 am. I basically found my phone and wallet in the car and called my business partner at 7:30 am and told him I had been kidnapped and most of our money from our business account was taken. He told me to call the police, so I did."

Explanation: The author uses five Pivot Words, possibly to avoid commitment to his statement. Did you notice that most of the Pivot Words are near the Occurrence of Significance. Did that strike you as interesting?

Irrelevant Information

> "I left my business at 8:30 pm and went to the Suds & Stuff Car Wash located at the <u>corner of Penn and Wright streets and across from Ponzi's donuts</u> [sometime] in the evening to clean and wash my car. ~~I just purchased it last month and it is <u>ruby red with gold pin stripes and has a 500 horse power engine</u>. I never race it on the streets because that would be a stupid thing to do. I know people who do that and they get themselves into trouble~~. It was 9:00 pm and ~~no one else was there~~ [probably] ~~because, in my opinion, of all the crime that happens there~~. Next, I started vacuuming the car. I was forced to lay face down on the back floor as my kidnappers drove me. I [guess] they took my wallet. Later, they had me make numerous withdrawals from my bank account. This [probably] lasted all night. Next thing you know I'm alone in my car at 5:30 am. I [basically] found my phone and wallet in the car and called my business partner at 7:30 am and told him I had been kidnapped and most of our money from our business account was taken. He told me to call the police, so I did."

Explanation: This statement has three examples of Irrelevant Information:

The first instance is where the victim describes his car. He may do this to lengthen his statement and give the impression that he is cooperating with the investigation.

The second is where he says he would never race his car on the streets. He may have inserted this Irrelevant Information to create a positive impression of himself as someone who is mindful of the law.

The third instance is where he describes the area where the carwash is located as dangerous, perhaps to explain *why* the kidnapping happened rather than *what* happened.

Time Markers

> "I left my business at 8:30 pm and went to the Suds & Stuff Car Wash located at the corner of Penn and Wright streets and across from Ponzi's donuts sometime in the evening to clean and wash my car. ~~I just purchased it last month and it is ruby red with gold pin stripes and has a 600 horse power engine. I never race it on the streets because that would be a stupid thing to do. I know people who do that and they get themselves into trouble.~~ It was 9:00 pm and ~~no one else was there~~ probably ~~because, in my opinion, of all the crime that happens there~~. Next, I started vacuuming the car. I was forced to lay face down on the back floor as my kidnappers drove me. I guess they took my wallet. Later, they had me make numerous withdrawals from my bank account. This probably lasted all night. Next thing you know I'm alone in my car at 5:30 am. I basically found my phone and wallet in the car and called my business partner at 7:30 am and told him I had been kidnapped and most of our money from our business account was taken. He told me to call the police, so I did."

Explanation: In his statement the victim uses four Time Markers. This is the timeline of his activities:

- 30 minutes to go to the carwash.
- 510 minutes to start vacuuming his car and then drive around with kidnappers to banks.
- 120 minutes to find his wallet and phone in the car, and to call his business partner.

The 510 minutes dedicated to starting to vacuum his car and then to be driven around by the kidnappers is concerning; as is the 120 minutes he takes to find his phone and wallet and then call his business partner.

What are the details for what happened during all those missing hours? Did something else occur?

SUMMARY

Based on the results using these methodologies, the investigator should recognize that much of the statement is not consistent with commitment. The investigator should now re-interview the victim to determine why his statement lacks commitment. Does the victim not show commitment to his statement because he is trying to protect his knowledge of what really happened?

CHAPTER 8: STATEMENT GAPS

This chapter discusses Statement Gaps and answers these three questions:
  • What are Statement Gaps?
  • How do we recognize Statement Gaps in a statement?
  • What do Statement Gaps tell us about an author's commitment to a statement?

Statement Gaps are sudden, unexpected breaks or interruptions in a statement that indicate an author's possible intention to skip over part of a statement. They can occur anywhere in a statement and examiners should take care not to overlook them and miss a vital indicator of omitted information.

Recognizing Statement Gaps is fairly simple. Keep in mind that when someone tells a story it usually flows logically from one activity or event to another. For example, if you ask someone to tell you what they did during their morning, they might say, "I took a shower, brushed my teeth, and got dressed. I then went to the store and bought a gallon of milk. I went home and ate some cereal. I then bathed my dog and after that I finished my morning by watching TV." The activities in the statement link together logically to create a free-flowing, uninterrupted statement.

In contrast, a Statement Gap will typically show up as a sudden break or disruption in a statement's flow of activities. It will make the statement appear clumsy. If you ask someone to

"No lie can live forever."

-Dr. Martin Luther King Jr

tell you what they did during their morning, they might say instead, "I took a shower. I returned from the store and I ate some cereal. I then bathed my dog and after that I finished my morning by watching TV." There is an obvious disruption in this statement's flow, a chasm or gap between the point when the author says he took a shower and when he says he returned from the store. People do not take a shower one moment and then suddenly find themselves returning from a store. Did the person giving the statement have guilty knowledge and leap over that part? Was the author involved in some activity he didn't want exposed?

Another example: An investigator suspects a husband of hitting his wife and asks him to tell him what happened. The husband says, "We got home from the ballet recital and had dinner. All of us then watched a movie about a space alien named B-Cubed. After the movie, we bathed the kids, had them brush their teeth, took them to their bedrooms, read books to them, and put them to bed. My wife then exited the garage and called the police."

Did you see the Statement Gap? It's between when the husband says he and his wife put the kids to bed and when he says his wife exited the garage. It's as if she has super powers–one moment she's putting the kids to bed and the next she's exiting the garage. The investigator should consider the possibility that the husband created a Statement Gap to avoid providing information about what actually happened after the children went to bed.

EXAMPLES

Mark a Statement Gap by writing the word *[GAP]* in brackets.

Question	Statement Gap	Observations
What did you do at the baseball game?	"I got to the stadium just in time. *[GAP]* On the way home I stopped for a pizza at Rudy's Sweet Tea Shack. Then I drove home."	The author does not explain what happened at the baseball game.
What did you do at school today?	"I had a test in the morning, followed by history and English, and then I ate lunch. *[GAP]* I took the bus home at 4:50pm."	What happened between lunch and taking the bus at 4:50pm?
What did you do on each day of your vacation?	"It was great. Each day was so much fun. We went to the museum on Monday. On Tuesday we took a cruise and went to a show. On Wednesday we went to the parade. *[GAP]* We got home on Saturday."	What happened on Thursday and Friday?

Chapter 8: Statement Gaps

Question	Statement Gap	Observations
What happened at the carnival?	"It was incredible! *[GAP]* At the movies we saw Attack of the Little Bloodsucker Scorpions and had drinks and popcorn. We then came home."	What happened at the carnival?
What caused your crash?	"I was driving on Sellman Avenue when I saw traffic backed up at the traffic light. *[GAP]* The officer gave me a ticket for not paying attention. I'm taking it to court!"	What happened between the author seeing the traffic and getting the ticket?
What did you and your boyfriend do while I was away?	"We studied two calculus chapters for our test. Then we decided to feed Fido and walk him around the block. *[GAP]* You arrived while I was in the shower."	What happened after they decided to walk Fido? Note that deciding to do something and actually doing something are two different things.
What did you between when you got home from work and when you returned from Lucky's house?	"Let's see ... I got home and ate a sandwich and chips. I also drank a soda. Then I took a shower and got dressed. *[GAP]* I got back home at 11pm."	A gap appears between when the author finishes dressing and when he returns from Lucky's.
What happened at Pam's party?	"I drove there, had a few beers with Al, played some ping-pong and drank a few more beers. Then I turned on the football game. *[GAP]* I got home, brushed my teeth and went to bed."	Why did the author skip what happened between the football game and his arriving home?

PRACTICE EXERCISES

EXERCISE 1

This statement is from a teenager whose parents ask him about a strange odor emanating from his clothes. They ask him where he was during the previous two hours. **Write [GAP] where you find a Statement Gap**.

> "When I got home from school, I went to the park to practice baseball with Greg, Mark, Kenny, Danny, and the rest of the team. Go ask them. In fact, why don't you call them. Here's my phone. Text them if you want. Practice lasted about an hour and then we walked to the creek and followed the path to Danny's house. His mom made us smoothies and we played some video games. Why don't you text her too, if you don't believe me. After I left, I met Jesse on the creek path. I took a shower, and here I am now being interrogated about nothing at all. I have my rights!"

Answer:

> "When I got home from school, I went to the park to practice baseball with Greg, Mark, Kenny, Danny, and the rest of the team. Go ask them. In fact, why don't you call them. Here's my phone. Text them if you want. Practice lasted about an hour and then we walked to the creek and followed the path to Danny's house. His mom made us smoothies and we played some video games. Why don't you text her too, if you don't believe me. After I left, I met Jesse on the creek path. *[GAP]* I took a shower, and here I am now being interrogated about nothing at all. I have my rights!"

Explanation: The gap is between where the author says he meets Jesse and where he says he takes a shower. Did Jesse and he do something? Did he continue to walk home? How did he get home? What happened when he got home? Did he do something before he showered? Could the Statement Gap indicate intent to avoid exposing guilty information? Did you notice that the son challenged his parents to confirm his story with his friends and with Danny's mom but he did not do the same with Jesse?

EXERCISE 2

This is the previous carwash kidnapping statement. **Write *[GAP]* where you find a Statement Gap**.

> "I left my business at 8:30 pm and went to the Suds & Stuff Car Wash located at the corner of Penn and Wright streets and across from Ponzi's donuts sometime in the evening to clean and wash my car. I just purchased it last month and it is ruby red with gold pin stripes and has a 500 horse power engine. I never race it on the streets because that would be a stupid thing to do. I know people who do that and they get themselves into trouble. It was 9:00 pm and no one else was there probably because, in my opinion, of all the crime that happens there. Next, I started vacuuming the car. *[GAP]* I was forced to lay face down on the back floor as my kidnappers drove me. I guess they took my wallet. Later, they had me make numerous withdrawals from my bank account. This probably lasted all night. *[GAP]* Next thing you know I'm alone in my car at 5:30 am. I basically found my phone and wallet in the car and called my business partner at 7:30 am and told him I had been kidnapped and most of our money from our business account was taken. He told me to call the police, so I did."

Answer:

> "I left my business at 8:30 pm and went to the Suds & Stuff Car Wash located at the corner of Penn and Wright streets and across from Ponzi's donuts sometime in the evening to clean and wash my car. I just purchased it last month and it is ruby red with gold pin stripes and has a 500 horse power engine. I never race it on the streets because that would be a stupid thing to do. I know people who do that and they get themselves into trouble. It was 9:00 pm and no one else was there probably because, in my opinion, of all the crime that happens there. Next, I started vacuuming the car. *[GAP]* I was forced to lay face down on the back floor as my kidnappers drove me. I guess they took my wallet. Later, they had me make numerous withdrawals from my bank account. This probably lasted all night. Next thing you know I'm alone in my car at 5:30 am. I basically found my phone and wallet in the car and called my business partner at 7:30 am and told him I had been kidnapped and most of our money from our business account was taken. He told me to call the police, so I did."

Explanation: The statement has one gap, between when he says he started vacuuming his car and when he says he is being forced to lay face down. How did he get kidnapped? What did the kidnappers look like? What did the kidnappers do to force him to lay down?

Did the words *next*, *later*, and *next thing you know* catch your attention? You may have considered them Statement Gaps and marked them accordingly. They are not Statement Gaps, but they are closely related. They are called Gap Cover Words because they help an author to conceal large breaks in a statement rather than leaving an awkwardly abrupt gap. We'll take a closer look at Gap Cover Words in the next chapter.

TIPS

TIP 1   **LOOK FOR SUDDEN STARTS AND STOPS**

Areas within a statement that appear disjointed or seem to suddenly stop and start are often good indicators of Statement Gaps.

TIP 2   **YOU MAY FIND MULTIPLE GAPS**

Some statements may contain more than one gap; not often, but it does happen.

TIP 3   **GAP LOCATION IS IMPORTANT**

Statement Gaps can be found anywhere in a statement. They are particularly interesting when they occur in or around the Occurrence of Significance.

TIP 4   **SOME STATEMENTS DO NOT CONTAIN GAPS**

In fact, many don't. Why? Some people simply don't have gaps in their story.

TIP 5   **STATEMENT GAPS DON'T ALWAYS INDICATE GUILTY KNOWLEDGE**

The presence of a Statement Gap does not necessarily show someone is manipulating a statement or trying to protect guilty knowledge. However, all Statement Gaps found within in a statement should be explored with the statement's author to determine if it is possibly being used as a strategy to avoid exposing information they don't want to share.

COMPREHENSIVE EXERCISE 5

This exercise covers all the previous methodologies. The statement is from a woman who says she was attacked on her way to work. Investigators ask her to describe what happened.

> "I was driving to work and I got caught in traffic because of the protest in front of the university. The traffic report said the protest would end in two hours, so I decided to wait it out at a coffee shop I occasionally go to at Village Squire Mall. While driving to the coffee shop, as best as I can recall, I think I drove on Lincoln Avenue and probably through Washington Circle to another street. I then stopped at a light located somewhere around the university. As I waited for the light to change, a group of what appeared to be protestors walked up and looked at me and one of them yelled and pointed at me. I drove myself to the hospital, they made me wait. I got tired of waiting and left. I am so lucky nothing serious happened. When I left the hospital, I called my boss at work and he told me to not come in and just go home and rest. In my opinion these protestors should not be allowed anywhere near the university because it causes too many problems for people such as me."

Steps

1. Draw a [box around] the Occurrence of Significance.
   Calculate the proportion here: _____
2. <u>Underline</u> any High-Quality Sensory Details.
3. <u>Underline</u> any High-Quality Locational Details.
4. Draw a [box] around any Pivot Words.
5. ~~Mark through~~ any Irrelevant Information.
6. Draw a (circle) around any Time Markers.
7. Write *[GAP]* where you find any Statement Gaps.

(Turn page for answers.)

ANSWERS

Occurrence of Significance

> "I was driving to work and I got caught in traffic because of the protest in front of the university. The traffic report said the protest would end in two hours, so I decided to wait it out at a coffee shop I occasionally go to at Village Squire Mall. While driving to the coffee shop, as best as I can recall, I think I drove on Lincoln Avenue and probably through Washington Circle to another street. I then stopped at a light located somewhere around the university. As I waited for the light to change, a group of what appeared to be protestors walked up and looked at me and ⟦one of them yelled and pointed at me⟧ I drove myself to the hospital, they made me wait. I got tired of waiting and left. I am so lucky nothing serious happened. When I left the hospital, I called my boss at work and he told me to not come in and just go home and rest. In my opinion these protestors should not be allowed anywhere near the university because it causes too many problems for people such as me."

Explanation: The Occurrence of Significance in this statement is only eight words out of the total 191 words in her statement—or approximately 4 percent. This reflects a lack of commitment by the author.

High-Quality Sensory & Locational Details

There are no High-Quality Sensory or Locational Details in this statement.

Pivot Words

> "I was driving to work and I got caught in traffic because of the protest in front of the university. The traffic report said the protest would end in two hours, so I decided to wait it out at a coffee shop I occasionally go to at Village Squire Mall. While driving to the coffee shop, ⟨as best as I can recall,⟩ I ⟨think⟩ I drove on Lincoln Avenue and ⟨probably⟩ through Washington Circle to another street. I then stopped at a light located ⟨somewhere⟩ ⟨around⟩ the university. As I waited for the light to change, a group of ⟨what⟩ ⟨appeared⟩ to be protestors walked up and looked at me and ⟨one of them yelled and pointed at me⟩ I drove myself to the hospital, they made me wait. I got tired of waiting and left. I am so lucky nothing serious happened. When I left the hospital, I called my boss at work and he told me to not come in and just go home and rest. In my opinion these protestors should not be allowed anywhere near the university because it causes too many problems for people such as me."

Explanation: The woman uses these Pivot Words possibly to avoid commitment and to pivot away from guilty information she may have about what happened with the protestors.

Irrelevant Information

> "~~I was driving to work and I got caught in traffic because of the protest in front of the university. The traffic report said the protest would end in two hours, so I decided to wait it out at a coffee shop I occasionally go to at Village Squire Mall. While driving to the coffee shop,~~ ⟨as best as I can recall,⟩ I ⟨think⟩ ~~I drove on Lincoln Avenue and~~ ⟨probably⟩ ~~through Washington Circle to another street. I then stopped at a light located~~ ⟨somewhere⟩ ⟨around⟩ ~~the university.~~ As I waited for the light to change, a group of ⟨what⟩ ⟨appeared⟩ to be protestors walked up and looked at me and ⟨one of them yelled and pointed at me⟩ I drove myself to the hospital, ~~they made me wait. I got tired of waiting and left. I am so lucky nothing serious happened. When I left the hospital, I called my boss at work and he told me to not come in and just go home and rest. In my opinion these protestors should not be allowed anywhere near the university because it causes too many problems for people such as me.~~"

Explanation: The victim uses Irrelevant Information throughout her statement–about two-thirds of it. Investigators ask her to describe *what* happened regarding the attack and she instead explains *why* the attack happened. She adds additional Irrelevant Information at the end of her statement when she mentions her luck and expresses her opinion about the protesters.

Time Markers

There is one instance of a Time Marker–the words "two hours"–but because there are no other references to time to give it context, this is insignificant.

Statement Gaps

> "~~I was driving to work and I got caught in traffic because of the protest in front of the university. The traffic report said the protest would end in two hours, so I decided to wait it out at a coffee shop I occasionally go to at Village Squire Mall. While driving to the coffee shop,~~ [as best as I can recall,] ~~I~~ [think] ~~I drove on Lincoln Avenue and~~ [probably] ~~through Washington Circle to another street. I then stopped at a light located~~ [somewhere] ~~around~~ ~~the university.~~ As I waited for the light to change, a group of what [appeared] to be protesters walked up and looked at me and [one of them yelled and pointed at me.] *[GAP]* I drove myself to the hospital, ~~they made me wait. I got tired of waiting and left. I am so lucky nothing serious happened. When I left the hospital, I called my boss at work and he told me to not come in and just go home and rest. In my opinion these protesters should not be allowed anywhere near the university because it causes too many problems for people such as me.~~"

Explanation: The Statement Gap is between where the author mentions a protester yelling and pointing at her and where she says she drove herself to the hospital.

SUMMARY

This statement clearly lacks commitment from the author. Could she be using the Statement Gap to avoid providing specifics about the attack because it never happened? The statement examiner should consider re-interviewing the victim with an emphasis on determining specifics about the attack.

CHAPTER 9: GAP COVER WORDS

This chapter explains the role of Gap Cover Words and answers these three questions:
- What is a Gap Cover Word?
- How do we recognize Gap Cover Words in a statement?
- What does a Gap Cover Word indicate about an author's commitment to their statement?

The last chapter covered Statement Gaps—conspicuous gaps in a statement that may indicate an author's intent to skip information. Gap Cover Words can conceal those gaps so they appear less obvious.

Consider this statement given by the victim of a mugging: "I was walking along Elm Street to the Sugarland Shack Palace when I saw two men approach me with their fists raised. I got up, rubbed my jaw, ran away and called the police." The Statement Gap is obvious in this example—a definite break in the statement between when the two men raised their fists and when the victim got up. You would write *[GAP]* there.

Now look at the same statement, but this time with a Gap Cover Word: "I was walking along Elm Street to the Sugarland Shack Palace when I saw two men approach me with their fists raised. Afterward, I got up, rubbed my jaw, ran away and called the police."

In this example, the word *afterward* covers the Statement Gap, making it appear less obvious. The author may have strategically concealed the truth by using a Gap Cover Word.

> *"The truth stays in the undergrowth, waiting to be discovered."*
> – Josephine Hart

EXAMPLES

Draw <angle brackets> around Gap Cover Words.

Question	Gap Cover Words	Observations
What happened last night?	"I drove to Mike's, had a few beers and played basketball. <Later> I started for home. <Next> I went to sleep."	What happened between playing basketball and starting home? And between starting home and going to sleep?
What happened on your trip to the mall?	"I bought a dress at Maude's Cirque Checker Shop. <Next> I ate lunch at Honey Dew Grill and went home."	*Next* fills the gap between the dress shop and eating lunch. What happened in that time?
What happened?	"We left the museum, got on the elevator and took it down to lobby. We <subsequently> got home and watched a video. <Next> the cops arrived and asked questions."	What happened between the elevator ride and getting home? What happened between watching the video and the cops arriving?
How was the opera?	"The opera started at 3:00. <Afterward> we began our journey home. "	What happened after the opera started? What is *afterward*– right after the opera or sometime later?
What did you do last night with your friends?	"We went to the bowling alley and <subsequently> got home around 11:00."	*Subsequently* covers up what happened between bowling and getting home.
What caused your burns?	"I started the grill for dinner. <A short time later> I put out the fire on my arm and went to the hospital."	What happened between starting the grill and putting out the fire?
What did you and Diane do while I was away?	"We watched a movie. <Sometime after that> I dropped her off at her home."	What happened between watching a movie and dropping off Diane?
What happened from the time you got ready for football practice until you got home?	"I got dressed, walked to the park, and the <next thing I knew> I was home at 8 pm."	What happened between the walk to the park and getting home? Did this person even attend practice?

PRACTICE EXERCISES

EXERCISE 1

A school's security officer suspects a girl of pulling the fire alarm and asks her to recount everything she did from when she went to the restroom to when she went outside. **Draw angle brackets around any Gap Cover Words**.

> "My name is Char Fyre. I am an honor student at Ember Burns High School. Just after lunch I went to English class. We were starting to read MacBeth and the teacher told us to stop because she needed us to first turn in our homework assignment that was due today. That was too bad because I really wanted to read some Shakespeare. He is my favorite author of all time. Faulkner is close, but I really do like Shakespeare, a lot. In fact, my English teacher told me she was impressed with my interest in the classics. Anyway, as I started to reach for my homework assignment to turn it in, I felt the urge to go to the bathroom. I asked Ms. Pros if I could go and she gave me permission. I went to the bathroom and the next thing I knew I was walking outside."

Answer:

> "My name is Char Fyre. I am an honor student at Ember Burns High School. Just after lunch I went to English class. We were starting to read MacBeth and the teacher told us to stop because she needed us to first turn in our homework assignment that was due today. That was too bad because I really wanted to read some Shakespeare. He is my favorite author of all time. Faulkner is close, but I really do like Shakespeare, a lot. In fact, my English teacher told me she was impressed with my interest in the classics. Anyway, as I started to reach for my homework assignment to turn it in, I felt the urge to go to the bathroom. I asked Ms. Pros if I could go and she gave me permission. I went to the bathroom and the <next thing I knew> I was walking outside."

Explanation: The student never explains what happened between the bathroom and going outside. What happened on her way to the bathroom? Did she make it to the bathroom? Did she hear the alarm? Did you also notice a lot of Irrelevant Information? What could this mean?

EXERCISE 2

Looking back at the carwash kidnapping statement again. Review the statement and this time **draw angle brackets around any Gap Cover Words**.

> "I left my business at 8:30 pm and went to the Suds & Stuff Car Wash located at the corner of Penn and Wright streets and across from Ponzi's donuts sometime in the evening to clean and wash my car. I just purchased it last month and it is ruby red with gold pin stripes and a 500 horse power engine. I never race it on the streets because that would be a stupid thing to do. I know people who do that and they get themselves into trouble. It was 9:00 pm and no one else was there probably because, in my opinion, of all the crime in that happens there. Next, I started vacuuming the car. I was forced to lay face down on the back floor as my kidnappers drove me. I guess they took my wallet. Later, they had me make numerous withdrawals from my bank account. This probably lasted all night. Next thing you know I'm alone in my car at 5:30 am. I basically found my phone and wallet in the car and called my business partner at 7:30 am and told him I had been kidnapped and most of our money from our business account was taken. He told me to call the police, so I did."

Chapter 9: Gap Cover Words

Answer:

> "I left my business at 8:30 pm and went to the Suds & Stuff Car Wash located at the corner of Penn and Wright streets and across from Ponzi's donuts sometime in the evening to clean and wash my car. I just purchased it last month and it is ruby red with gold pin stripes and a 500 horse power engine. I never race it on the streets because that would be a stupid thing to do. I know people who do that and they get themselves into trouble. It was 9:00 pm and no one else was there probably because, in my opinion, of all the crime in that happens there. <Next>, I started vacuuming the car. I was forced to lay face down on the back floor as my kidnappers drove me. I guess they took my wallet. <Later>, they had me make numerous withdrawals from my bank account. This probably lasted all night. <Next thing you know> I'm alone in my car at 5:30 am. I basically found my phone and wallet in the car and called my business partner at 7:30 am and told him I had been kidnapped and most of our money from our business account was taken. He told me to call the police, so I did."

Explanation: There are three instances of Gap Cover Words in this statement. The first is the word *next* that covers the gap between getting to the carwash and starting to vacuum. Could something have occurred between these two activities that the author does not want to share? The second Gap Cover Word, *later*, covers the gap between the kidnappers taking his wallet and having him make bank withdrawals. Did something happen in that interval? The last instance is the phrase *next thing you know*, which covers the gap between driving around all night and finding himself alone his car. What happened in that time?

TIPS

TIP 1 **ASK QUESTIONS**

If you are unsure if the word or words you identified in a statement are Gap Cover Words, ask yourself these two questions. If you agree with the questions you likely have identified a Gap Cover Word.
• Does the word or group of words cover a Statement Gap?
• If you remove the Gap Words from the statement, are you left with any abrupt Statement Gaps?

TIP 2 **GAP COVER WORDS ARE NOT PROOF**

The absence or presence of Gap Cover Words in a statement should not lead an examiner to conclude the statement's author is hiding guilty information. The words should be noted and then explored with the statement's author to determine the intent in using them.

TIP 3 **LOOK FOR GAP COVER WORDS AT THE OCCURRENCE OF SIGNIFICANCE**

Gap cover words can be found almost anywhere in a statement. However, finding them in and around the Occurrence of Significance should raise the concern of the examiner.

TIP 4 **MOST GAP COVER WORDS ARE ADVERBS OR ADVERBIAL PHRASES**

COMPREHENSIVE EXERCISE 6

This exercise covers all the methodologies we've learned so far. In this incident, a woman hears a gunshot from Mr. Boom's house and calls the police. The police respond to Mr. Boom's house and ask him what happened.

> "Okay, I was like cleaning my gun as I usually do. I sort of got out my brushes, patches, cleaner, rags, and gun oil. I noticed my gun oil was getting low and I made a note to buy some more on my phone. I unloaded my gun and disassembled it (it was a new one I had bought a few months ago and had used it only twice). With everything set up, I started cleaning it. It was kind of dirty and it probably took a few minutes to clean it. I cleaned it to my satisfaction and put it back together. Joe called and asked if I was watching the game because it was really exciting.
>
> I turned on the tv and we were up by two points, which is crazy because we hadn't beaten a ranked team since forever. Toward the end of the game, they let the other team drive down the field and score a field goal with one second left. Of course, we couldn't do anything on the ensuing kickoff, so we lost the game as usual. I may have been holding the gun at this point.
>
> I subsequently heard a loud boom and it now looks like there's possibly a hole in my new tv."

Steps

1. Draw a |box around| the Occurrence of Significance.
   Calculate the proportion here:
2. <u>Underline</u> any High-Quality Sensory Details.
3. <u>Underline</u> any High-Quality Locational Details.
4. Draw a |box| around any Pivot Words.
5. ~~Mark through~~ any Irrelevant Information.
6. Draw a (circle) around any Time Markers.
7. Write ***[GAP]*** where you find any Statement Gaps.
8. Draw <angle brackets> around any Gap Cover Words.

(Turn page for answers.)

ANSWERS

Occurrence of Significance

> "Okay, I was like cleaning my gun as I usually do. I sort of got out my brushes, patches, cleaner, rags, and gun oil. I noticed my gun oil was getting low and I made a note to buy some more on my phone. I unloaded my gun and disassembled it (it was a new one I had bought a few months ago and had used it only twice). With everything set up, I started cleaning it. It was kind of dirty and it probably took a few minutes to clean it. I cleaned it to my satisfaction and put it back together. Joe called and asked if I was watching the game because it was really exciting.
>
> I turned on the tv and we were up by two points, which is crazy because we hadn't beaten a ranked team since forever. Toward the end of the game, they let the other team drive down the field and score a field goal with one second left. Of course, we couldn't do anything on the ensuing kickoff, so we lost the game as usual. I may have been holding the gun at this point.
>
> I subsequently ⟦heard a loud boom⟧ and it now looks like there's possibly a hole in my new tv."

Explanation: Mr. Boom uses four words in his 202-word statement that cover the Occurrence of Significance. That is only 2 percent of the overall statement. Remember, he was asked to explain what happened, not everything he did from the time he started cleaning his gun until the time he saw the hole in his TV.

Comprehensive Exercise 6

High-Quality Sensory & Locational Details

> "Okay, I was like cleaning my gun as I usually do. I sort of got out my brushes, patches, cleaner, rags, and gun oil. I noticed my gun oil was getting low and I made a note to buy some more on my phone. I unloaded my gun and disassembled it (it was a new one I had bought a few months ago and had used it only twice). With everything set up, I started cleaning it. It was kind of dirty and it probably took a few minutes to clean it. I cleaned it to my satisfaction and put it back together. Joe called and asked if I was watching the game because it was really exciting.
>
> I turned on the tv and we were up by two points, which is crazy because we hadn't beaten a ranked team since forever. Toward the end of the game, they let the other team drive down the field and score a field goal with one second left. Of course, we couldn't do anything on the ensuing kickoff, so we lost the game as usual. I may have been holding the gun at this point.
>
> I subsequently [heard a loud boom] and it now looks like there's possibly a hole in my new tv."

Explanation: The loud boom is the only High-Quality Sensory Detail. There are no High-Quality Locational Details.

Pivot Words

> "Okay, I was [like] cleaning my gun as I usually do. I [sort of] got out my brushes, patches, cleaner, rags, and gun oil. I noticed my gun oil was getting low and I made a note to buy some more on my phone. I unloaded my gun and disassembled it (it was a new one I had bought a [few] months ago and had used it only twice). With everything set up, I started cleaning it. It was [kind of] dirty and it [probably] took a [few] minutes to clean it. I cleaned it to my satisfaction and put it back together. Joe called and asked if I was watching the game because it was really exciting.
>
> I turned on the tv and we were up by two points, which is crazy because we hadn't beaten a ranked team since forever. Toward the end of the game, they let the other team drive down the field and score a field goal with one second left. Of course, we couldn't do anything on the ensuing kickoff, so we lost the game as usual. [I may have been] holding the gun at this point.
>
> I subsequently [heard a loud boom] and it now looks [like] there's [possibly] a hole in my new tv."

Explanation: This statement has nine Pivot Words or phrases. One phrase is especially concerning. Did you find it? It's *may have been* toward the end of his statement. Was he or was he not holding the gun?

Irrelevant Information

> "Okay, I was ~~like~~ cleaning my gun as I usually do. ~~I sort of got out my brushes, patches, cleaner, rags, and gun oil. I noticed my gun oil was getting low and I made a note to buy some more on my phone. I unloaded my gun and disassembled it (it was a new one I had bought a few months ago and had used it only twice). With everything set up, I started cleaning it. It was kind of dirty and it probably took a few minutes to clean it. I cleaned it to my satisfaction and put it back together. Joe called and asked if I was watching the game because it was really exciting.~~
>
> ~~I turned on the tv and we were up by two points, which is crazy because we hadn't beaten a ranked team since forever. Toward the end of the game, they let the other team drive down the field and score a field goal with one second left. Of course, we couldn't do anything on the ensuing kickoff, so we lost the game as usual.~~ I may have been holding the gun at this point.
>
> I subsequently heard a loud boom and it now looks like there's possibly a hole in my new tv."

Explanation: The man's statement is mainly Irrelevant Information, perhaps intended to conceal that he is not answering the question.

Time Markers

There are no Time Markers in the man's statement.

Statement Gaps

There are no Statement Gaps in the man's statement.

Gap Cover Words

> "Okay, I was [like] cleaning my gun as I usually do. ~~I [sort of] got out my brushes, patches, cleaner, rags, and gun oil. I noticed my gun oil was getting low and I made a note to buy some more on my phone. I unloaded my gun and disassembled it (it was a new one I had bought a [few] months ago and had used it only twice). With everything set up, I started cleaning it. It was [kind of] dirty and it [probably] took a [few] minutes to clean it. I cleaned it to my satisfaction and put it back together. Joe called and asked if I was watching the game because it was really exciting.~~
>
> ~~I turned on the tv and we were up by two points, which is crazy because we hadn't beaten a ranked team since forever. Toward the end of the game, they let the other team drive down the field and score a field goal with one second left. Of course, we couldn't do anything on the ensuing kickoff, so we lost the game as usual.~~ I [may have been] holding the gun at this point.
>
> I <subsequently> [heard a loud boom] and it now looks [like] there's [possibly] a hole in my new tv."

Explanation: There is one Gap Cover Word, *subsequently*, in the last sentence of his statement. The word covers the gap between the end of the game and the loud boom. He doesn't explain what caused his gun to fire. Surely something caused it to discharge; guns just don't go off by themselves!

SUMMARY

These methodologies show that Mr. Boom lacks commitment to his statement. The officer should consider the possibility that Mr. Boom is hiding guilty information, perhaps to avoid revealing what really happened. Did Mr. Boom get upset with his team's performance and shoot his own TV?

CHAPTER 10: UNCOMPLETED-ACTION WORDS

This chapter discusses Uncompleted-Action Words and answers these three questions:
- What is an Uncompleted-Action Word?
- How do you locate an Uncompleted-Action Word in a statement?
- What do Uncompleted-Action Words tell us about an author's commitment to their statement?

Similar to Gap Cover Words, Uncompleted-Action Words can allow an author to gloss over parts of a statement that they may prefer not to disclose. These types of words indicate the beginning of an action but not necessarily the end of an action. For instance, the Uncompleted-Action Word *started* indicates an action beginning but by itself does not indicate an action ending. The statement examiner should always take a close look at Uncompleted-Action Words and try to determine if the uncompleted action is completed later in the statement. If an action isn't completed, then the examiner should try to determine what happened.

Uncompleted-Action Words are effective because they can lull the reader or listener into assuming that any action begun is eventually completed, when in fact it may not have been.

An example is this statement: "It was time to get to the airport, so I collected my shoes, got my cosmetics together, checked to make sure the doors and windows were locked, and began packing my clothes. I then caught a cab for the airport and made my flight." The Uncompleted-Action Word *began*

> *"He who permits himself to tell a lie once, finds it much easier to do it the second time."*
>
> *– Thomas Jefferson*

allows the author to avoid committing to what happened between the time she started packing her clothes and when she catches a ride for the airport. An examiner could easily fail to catch the Uncompleted-Action Word and assume the action was completed. But was it? If so, why not say so? Was there something else that happened that was masked by the Uncompleted-Action Word? Keep in mind, when someone indicates they started something, there should also be an indication that they finished it.

Here is the same statement without the Uncompleted-Action Word: "It was time to get to the airport, so I collected my shoes, got my cosmetics together, checked to make sure the doors and windows were locked, and packed my clothes. I then caught a cab for the airport and made my flight." This statement flows better. The action of packing clothes is no longer pending–it is completed and the examiner should have no questions.

EXAMPLES

Draw (parentheses) around Uncompleted-Action Words.

Question	Uncompleted-Action Words	Observations
What did you do after you got home?	"I watched some TV, ate an apple and (proceeded) to bed."	Did the author go to bed? Why didn't he simply say he went to bed?
What happened?	"I walked into the store and this guy (began) to yell at me, so I decided to leave."	Did the guy ever stop yelling? What happened between the beginning of the yelling and the author leaving the store?
Did you do your homework?	"As soon as I got home I (started) my homework."	The author started the homework, but did they ever finish? Is the author hoping to send the message that they finished their homework?
Did you finish the project?	"We (initiated) the project at noon and went home a few hours later."	Did they finish the project? Is the word *initiated* used to trick the listener into assuming the project was completed? If the author finished the project, why didn't he simply say it was finished?
What did you do from the time you left work until the time you got home?	"I got in my car and drove to D-Gas where I filled up my tank. I paid for the gas and drove to the pharmacy. I bought some Tylenol and (started heading) to the barber shop. I got home and ate dinner."	The author said they *started heading* to the barber shop, but did he make it there, or did something else happen?

PRACTICE EXERCISES

EXERCISE 1

This statement is from a teenager suspected of vandalizing a recreation center. The investigator asks the teenager to account for his whereabouts at the time the center was vandalized. **Draw parentheses around any Uncompleted-Action Words**.

> "I was at my parent's house all night. I had friends over earlier and I'm pretty sure we played video games until nine. After that, we made some steak sandwiches and did stuff until about midnight. Then we played more video games and did other things, but we had to be quiet because it was getting late and my father is a real grouch about noise. So, out of respect for him I told my friends to leave at about somewhere around one. After they left, I started getting ready for bed and a couple of hours later the cops were at the door asking questions."

Answer:

> "I was at my parent's house all night. I had friends over earlier and I'm pretty sure we played video games until nine. After that, we made some steak sandwiches and did stuff until about midnight. Then we played more video games and did other things, but we had to be quiet because it was getting late and my father is a real grouch about noise. So, out of respect for him I told my friends to leave at about somewhere around one. After they left, I (started getting ready) for bed and a couple of hours later the cops were at the door asking questions."

Explanation: The teenager uses Uncompleted-Action Words when he says he *started getting ready* for bed. How does someone start getting ready for bed? Did he ever get in bed and go to sleep? Could the teenager be using Uncompleted-Action Words as a strategy to mask something else that happened?

Chapter 10: Uncompleted-Action Words

EXERCISE 2

A man is accused of hitting his wife with a bottle. An interviewer asks him to explain what happened. **Draw parentheses around any Uncompleted-Action Words**.

> "My wife had just come inside the house after spending all of her day on the beach. She commenced asking if I had been drinking. When she was finished with the interrogation, I said I hadn't been drinking. She started accusing me of smoking weed and when she was finished with that accusation I told her I had not. She began to go through the kitchen garbage can and when she was done, she had found a couple of beer cans. She said she now had proof that I had been drinking and that I was also a liar. She cried and said she was really upset because I had promised I wouldn't drink on vacation. I told her I was sorry and she said I wasn't. She stormed out of the kitchen and went into the bedroom and began going through my luggage until she came across a bottle of my favorite whiskey. Later, she pulled it out of my luggage and took it to the bathroom. I asked her what she was doing and she began to pour it out. Next, she told me our relationship was over and she was reporting me to the police. Then you guys showed up, heard her story, and arrested me for hitting her."

Answer:

> "My wife had just come inside the house after spending all of her day on the beach. She (commenced) asking if I had been drinking. When she was finished with the interrogation, I said I hadn't been drinking. She (started) accusing me of smoking weed and when she was finished with that accusation I told her I had not. She (began) to go through the kitchen garbage can and when she was done, she had found a couple of beer cans. She said she now had proof that I had been drinking and that I was also a liar. She cried and said she was really upset because I had promised I wouldn't drink on vacation. I told her I was sorry and she said I wasn't. She stormed out of the kitchen and went into the bedroom and (began) going through my luggage until she came across a bottle of my favorite whiskey. Later, she pulled it out of my luggage and took it to the bathroom. I asked her what she was doing and she (began) to pour it out. Next, she told me our relationship was over and she was reporting me to the police. Then you guys showed up, heard her story, and arrested me for hitting her."

Explanation: The man uses five Uncompleted-Action Words in his statement, however the first four are of little concern because the uncompleted actions they represent are subsequently completed. Of more concern is the final Uncompleted-Action Word when he says his wife *began* pouring out the whiskey. That action is not completed in his statement. Did his wife finish pouring out the whiskey? Did something happen at that point that encouraged the man to mask his actions with an Uncompleted-Action Word?

TIPS

TIP 1 DON'T MAKE ASSUMPTIONS ABOUT USAGE

If someone uses Uncompleted-Action Words in a statement, that does not necessarily indicate they are trying to avoid explaining something they don't want to explain. The statement examiner should always consider the possibility that Uncompleted-Action Words are an authentic part of the author's communication baseline. To understand why any Uncompleted-Action Words are used, an examiner should always try to re-interview the statement's author to determine if they were using the Uncompleted-Action Words to avoid revealing guilty information.

TIP 2 LOOK FOR UNCOMPLETED-ACTION WORDS NEAR THE OCCURRENCE OF SIGNIFICANCE

Uncompleted-Action Words can be located anywhere in a statement. However, finding them in or around an Occurrence of Significance is especially concerning.

TIP 3 UNCOMPLETED-ACTION WORDS ARE USUALLY VERBS

Almost all Uncompleted-Action Words are verbs. That does not mean all verbs are Uncompleted-Action Words, just those that are related to an action that is not subsequently completed.

COMPREHENSIVE EXERCISE 7

This exercise covers all of the previous methodologies. A rail-yard employee is suspected of stealing goods from a rail car during his shift. An officer asks him what he did during his shift.

> "I came into work at 12:00 am and walked the yard as I normally do. I checked out a walkie-talkie, a flashlight, a night stick and handcuffs. We love having these items on patrol because we sometimes run across some bad characters breaking into cars. Just last month we had two incidents of people trying to break into some cars on the north end of the yard. I personally caught one of them. It's really crazy out there these days. On a typical shift I cover two rail lines and the perimeter fence three times per night. There are two guards on duty during each 12:00 am – 8:00 am shift. On the night of the theft, I was on duty with John Evans. He has two-years of experience and I have three. At the start of my shift John went his way (lines 3 and 4) and I went my way (lines 1 and 2). I checked the doors on all the cars on line 1. I followed that by checking the perimeter and then I checked the doors on all the cars on line 2. It was all good. During my second round, I checked the doors on all the cars on line 1 again. I followed that by checking the perimeter again and then I checked the doors on all the cars on line 2 again. Following that I initiated my third round. I was called at home a few hours later and was asked to come back because there was a problem discovered by the day shift security on line 2."

Steps

1. Draw a [box around] the Occurrence of Significance.
    Calculate the proportion here:
2. <u>Underline</u> any High-Quality Sensory Details.
3. <u>Underline</u> any High-Quality Locational Details.
4. Draw a [box] around any Pivot Words.
5. ~~Mark through~~ any Irrelevant Information.
6. Draw a (circle) around any Time Markers.
7. Write *[GAP]* where you find any Statement Gaps.
8. Draw <angle brackets> around any Gap Cover Words.
9. Draw (parentheses) around any Uncompleted Action Words.

(Turn page for answers.)

ANSWERS

Occurrence of Significance

There is no Occurrence of Significance.

High-Quality Sensory & Locational Details

There are no High-Quality Sensory or Locational Details.

Pivot Words

> "I came into work at 12:00 am and walked the yard as I normally do. I checked out a walkie-talkie, a flashlight, a night stick and handcuffs. We love having these items on patrol because we ⌈sometimes⌉ run across ⌈some⌉ bad characters breaking into cars. Just last month we had two incidents of people trying to break into ⌈some⌉ cars on the north end of the yard. I personally caught one of them. It's really crazy out there these days. On a typical shift I cover two rail lines and the perimeter fence three times per night. There are two guards on duty during each 12:00 am – 8:00 am shift. On the night of the theft, I was on duty with John Evans. He has two-years of experience and I have three. At the start of my shift John went his way (lines 3 and 4) and I went my way (lines 1 and 2). I checked the doors on all the cars on line 1. I followed that by checking the perimeter and then I checked the doors on all the cars on line 2. It was all good. During my second round, I checked the doors on all the cars on line 1 again. I followed that by checking the perimeter again and then I checked the doors on all the cars on line 2 again. Following that I initiated my third round. I was called at home a ⌈few⌉ hours later and was asked to come back because there was a problem discovered by the day shift security on line 2."

Explanation: The statement contains four Pivot Words but because they do not appear to significantly allow the author to avoid commitment to his statement, they should not be considered as important.

Irrelevant Information

> "I came into work at 12:00 am and walked the yard ~~as I normally do~~. I checked out a walkie-talkie, a flashlight, a night stick and handcuffs. ~~We love having these items on patrol because we~~ sometimes ~~run across~~ some ~~bad characters breaking into cars. Just last month we had two incidents of people trying to break into~~ some ~~cars on the north end of the yard. I personally caught one of them. It's really crazy out there these days. On a typical shift I cover two rail lines and the perimeter fence three times per night. There are two guards on duty during each 12:00 am – 8:00 am shift~~. On the night of the theft, I was on duty with John Evans. ~~He has two years of experience and I have three~~. At the start of my shift John went his way (lines 3 and 4) and I went my way (lines 1 and 2). I checked the doors on all the cars on line 1. I followed that by checking the perimeter and then I checked the doors on all the cars on line 2. It was all good. During my second round, I checked the doors on all the cars on line 1 again. I followed that by checking the perimeter again and then I checked the doors on all the cars on line 2 again. Following that I initiated my third round. I was called at home a few hours later and was asked to come back because there was a problem discovered by the day shift security on line 2."

Explanation: The employee uses Irrelevant Information at the beginning and in the middle of his statement perhaps to create the perception that his job is dangerous, that he catches criminals just like a police officer, and that he has many years of experience doing it. By creating such a perception the author could be trying to ingratiate himself with the police officer.

Time Markers

> "I came into work at 12:00 am and walked the yard ~~as I normally do~~. I checked out a walkie-talkie, a flashlight, a night stick and handcuffs. ~~We love having these items on patrol because we sometimes run across some bad characters breaking into cars. Just last month we had two incidents of people trying to break into some cars on the north end of the yard. I personally caught one of them. It's really crazy out there these days. On a typical shift I cover two rail lines and the perimeter fence three times per night. There are two guards on duty during each 12:00 am – 8:00 am shift~~. On the night of the theft, I was on duty with John Evans. ~~He has two years of experience and I have three~~. At the start of my shift John went his way (lines 3 and 4) and I went my way (lines 1 and 2). I checked the doors on all the cars on line 1. I followed that by checking the perimeter and then I checked the doors on all the cars on line 2. It was all good. During my second round, I checked the doors on all the cars on line 1 again. I followed that by checking the perimeter again and then I checked the doors on all the cars on line 2 again. Following that I initiated my third round. I was called at home a few hours later and was asked to come back because there was a problem discovered by the day shift security on line 2."

Explanation: There are three Time Markers in this statement but they do not provide any significant results.

Statement Gaps

> "I came into work at ~~12:00 am~~ and walked the yard ~~as I normally do~~. I checked out a walkie-talkie, a flashlight, a night stick and handcuffs. ~~We love having these items on patrol because we sometimes run across some bad characters breaking into cars. Just last month we had two incidents of people trying to break into some cars on the north end of the yard. I personally caught one of them. It's really crazy out there these days. On a typical shift I cover two rail lines and the perimeter fence three times per night. There are two guards on duty during each~~ ~~12:00 am – 8:00 am shift~~. On the night of the theft, I was on duty with John Evans. ~~He has two years of experience and I have three.~~ At the start of my shift John went his way (lines 3 and 4) and I went my way (lines 1 and 2). I checked the doors on all the cars on line 1. I followed that by checking the perimeter and then I checked the doors on all the cars on line 2. It was all good. During my second round, I checked the doors on all the cars on line 1 again. I followed that by checking the perimeter again and then I checked the doors on all the cars on line 2 again. Following that I initiated my third round. *[GAP]* I was called at home a few hours later and was asked to come back because there was a problem discovered by the day shift security on line 2."

Explanation: This statement has one Statement Gap between when the man says he initiated his third round and when he says he received a call at home. In this case the statement examiner should be curious about the location of the Statement Gap and attempt to get details from the rail-yard employee about what he was doing from the time he began his third round until the time he received the phone call asking him to return to work.

Gap Cover Words

There are no Gap Cover Words.

Uncompleted-Action Words

> "I came into work at 12:00 am and walked the yard ~~as I normally do~~. I checked out a walkie-talkie, a flashlight, a night stick and handcuffs. ~~We love having these items on patrol because we sometimes run across some bad characters breaking into cars. Just last month we had two incidents of people trying to break into some cars on the north end of the yard. I personally caught one of them. It's really crazy out there these days. On a typical shift I cover two rail lines and the perimeter fence three times per night. There are two guards on duty during each 12:00 am – 8:00 am shift~~. On the night of the theft, I was on duty with John Evans. ~~He has two years of experience and I have three~~. At the (start) of my shift John went his way (lines 3 and 4) and I went my way (lines 1 and 2). I checked the doors on all the cars on line 1. I followed that by checking the perimeter and then I checked the doors on all the cars on line 2. It was all good. During my second round, I checked the doors on all the cars on line 1 again. I followed that by checking the perimeter again and then I checked the doors on all the cars on line 2 again. Following that I (initiated) my third round. *[GAP]* I was called at home a few hours later and was asked to come back because there was a problem discovered by the day shift security on line 2."

Explanation: The word *start* is an Uncompleted-Action Word. The employee says he started his shift but never indicates that he ended it. The employee also uses the word *initiated* to indicate he starts his third round, but does he ever complete that round? By using the Uncompleted-Action Word the employee could be trying to create the impression that he had completed the third round.

SUMMARY

This statement shows a possible lack of commitment because of the Irrelevant Information, the Statement Gap, and the Uncompleted Action Words. The responding police officer should re-interview the rail-yard employee to determine exactly what he did during his third round.

CHAPTER 11: NON-SPECIFIC TRANSIT WORDS

This chapter examines Non-Specific Transit Words and answers these three questions:
- What is a Non-Specific Transit Word?
- How do you recognize Non-Specific Transit Words in a statement?
- What do Non-Specific Transit Words tell us about an author's commitment to their statement?

Transit Words describe a method of transport and are typically in the form of one past-tense verb such as bicycled or cruised; or a multi-word combination of a past-tense verb and a noun, such as took a train or rode my motorcycle.

Transit Words can be an effective tool for minimizing the exposure of guilty knowledge. Transit Words can occur anywhere in a statement and examiners who are not careful can look past them and miss out on an indicator of omitted information. Transit Words are either specific or non-specific.

Specific Transit Words are found when a statement author identifies a specific mode of transit—for example in a car, on the subway, by walking, or on a plane. By using these specific Transit Words, the author is committed to a definite transportation type and to the related processes associated with that activity. For instance, when a person says they rode their bicycle, that involves commitment to the use of a bicycle. And also involves commitment to the related processes such as sitting on its seat, grabbing its handle bars, and pedaling.

"There is nothing more deceptive than an obvious fact."

– Sherlock Holmes

Likewise, when someone says they drove their car, that involves commitment to the use of a car and the related processes of getting in a car, fastening the safety belt, placing a hand on the steering wheel, starting it, putting it into gear, and accelerating down the road.

Non-Specific Transit Words are a vague and indefinite description of transit. For someone who wishes to avoid commitment to their mode of transportation, using Non-Specific Transit Words can be an appealing strategy. Take for example a woman without a driver's license who has driven herself to the hospital after shooting herself in the toe. She may not want to reveal that she drove a car without a license so when interviewed by police she may say, "I accidentally shot my toe, wrapped it in a blanket and made my way to the emergency room to get help." The non-specific Transit Words, *made my way*, allow the woman to avoid exposing her guilty information that she drove herself to the hospital without a license.

Specific Transit Words are preferable in a statement because specific words show commitment to both the type of transportation used and the related processes. These related processes can be investigated to corroborate a person's statement. For example, if someone says they flew to a city, that specific mode of transportation involves commitment to an airplane ride and to the related processes such as buying a ticket, checking baggage, walking through security, boarding a plane, sitting in a seat, and de-boarding the plane. All of these processes potentially can be confirmed or not confirmed through investigation.

If a person uses Non-Specific Transit Words, they may be attempting to conceal culpable information.

EXAMPLES: SPECIFIC TRANSIT WORDS

Question	Specific Transit Words
How did you get to school after you missed the bus?	"I biked to school."
Did you take a cab to the bar?	"No. Sheila drove me to the bar."
Did you take the train?	"No. I flew to the city."
Did you walk home from the concert?	"I rode the train home."
Did you walk with your friends to the museum?	"I took the subway to the museum."
How did you get to the office?	"I caught a cab."
How did you make it to the island?	"I took the ferry."

EXAMPLES: NON-SPECIFIC TRANSIT WORDS

Draw [brackets] around Non-Specific Transit Words in a statement

Question	Non-Specific Transit Words
How did you get here so fast?	"I [bolted]."
Did you go to Philip's house?	"I eventually [made my way] there."
What did you do after you left Philip's house?	"I [got to] the boardwalk and rode the roller coaster."
What did you do after the recital?	"I [found my way] to the park."
What did you do after dinner?	"I [skipped] over to the restaurant."
Where are your friends?	"They [dipped]."
Have you seen Lori?	"I [cruised] by her house tonight, but I didn't see her."
How did you get to the party?	"We were [out and about] and [ended up] there."
What did you do after getting the money?	"I [rabbited] to the liquor store."
What did you do after you heard the shots.	"I [jetted] home."
What did you and your friends do?	"We [split]."
What did you do after you were at the mall?	"I [went] home."
How did you get to the city?	"I [traveled] to the station and bought a ticket."
Did you do anything after the call?	"I [zipped] over."
Why did you leave in such a hurry?	"I [ran out] for burgers."
What did you do after you were chased by the man with the axe?	"I [rolled] to Joe's house."
What did you do when she gave you the property?	"I [dashed] to Nick's."
Where did you go after the speech?	"I [headed] to the school with the protestors."

PRACTICE EXERCISES

EXERCISE 1

A police officer is investigating a tip that a man who rode his motorcycle to a party the previous day had taken drugs to the party in the saddlebags of his motorcycle. The officer asks the man, "How did you get to party?" **Draw brackets around any Non-Specific Transit Words** in the mans's answer.

> "I heard there was a party at Weston Heights during my break at work. Everybody was talking about it, even the managers, so I knew it was going to be a good one! After I got off work, I thought about going and figured why not? It was Friday and I had a three-day weekend lined up, right? So, I thought I would hit this party. I took a shower, cleaned up, watched some tv, drank a few beers and made my way over. It was an excellent party. The DJ kept it going all night and everybody was cool, you know what I mean?"

Answer:

> "I heard there was a party at Weston Heights during my break at work. Everybody was talking about it, even the managers, so I knew it was going to be a good one! After I got off work, I thought about going and figured why not? It was Friday and I had a three-day weekend lined up, right? So, I thought I would hit this party. I took a shower, cleaned up, watched some tv, drank a few beers and [made my way over]. It was an excellent party. The DJ kept it going all night and everybody was cool, you know what I mean?"

Explanation: The officer should consider that the man used the words *made my way over* to avoid committing to how he got to the party.

EXERCISE 2

This statement is from a man suspected of stealing a purse on a public bus. The bus had just dropped the man off at a shopping mall as the theft was discovered. Inside the mall a police officer stops a person matching that man's description and asks him how he got to the mall. **Draw brackets around any Non-Specific Transit Words** in his statement.

> "Yesterday I was here at the mall looking for a new jacket. I found one at Less is More, but it was $300, so I didn't buy it. The salesperson said it would be $150 on Monday (today). So today when I woke up, I remembered it was Monday and I really wanted that jacket. So, after lunch I bolted over here. When I got here, I went to the store I told you about and they told me I was too late because someone else just bought it. I was disappointed and decided to keep looking and then you guys stopped me."

Answer:

> "Yesterday I was here at the mall looking for a new jacket. I found one at Less is More, but it was $300, so I didn't buy it. The salesperson said it would be $150 on Monday (today). So today when I woke up, I remembered it was Monday and I really wanted that jacket. So, after lunch I [bolted] over here. When I got here, I went to the store I told you about and they told me I was too late because someone else just bought it. I was disappointed and decided to keep looking and then you guys stopped me."

Explanation: Could the man be using the word *bolted* to avoid giving details about how he got to the mall? Could it have been by bus? In this case the interviewing police officer should repeat the question, emphasizing the need for specific information regarding how the man got to the mall.

TIPS

TIP 1   **NON-SPECIFIC TRANSIT WORDS MAY HIDE CULPABILITY**

Non-Specific Transit Words sometimes are used when a person is trying to avoid exposing guilty knowledge. Interviewers should explore these words to determine if the author is attempting to avoid commitment.

TIP 2   **NON-SPECIFIC TRANSIT WORDS DON'T ALWAYS HIDE CULPABILITY**

Non-Specific Transit Words don't necessarily indicate guilty knowledge and could simply be part of a person's natural communication baseline. When an author describes a non-specific mode of transit the interviewer should try to determine if the author can commit to a specific mode.

TIP 3   **LOOK FOR NON-SPECIFIC TRANSIT WORDS IN OR NEAR THE OCCURRENCE OF SIGNIFICANCE**

Transit Words can be located anywhere in a statement, but finding Non-Specific Transit Words in or around the Occurrence of Significance should be concerning to the statement examiner.

TIP 4   **TRANSIT WORDS ARE NOT ALWAYS FOUND IN STATEMENTS**

TIP 5   **SPECIFIC TRANSIT WORDS REFLECT COMMITMENT TO A STATEMENT**

A specific Transit Word is a specific description of how a person moved from one point to another and reflects commitment. A Non-Specific Transit Word does the opposite—it is a vague description of transit and reflects a lack of commitment.

FINAL COMPREHENSIVE EXERCISE

This final comprehensive exercise examines a statement using all of the methodologies in this book. The statement is from a young woman whose parents suspect she used their sports car and damaged it while they were out of town. The parents ask their daughter how the car was damaged.

> "Let's see ... you left here and I did the dishes and stuff, and other things like that. I walked to Zack's located across the street from the Kingston Park entrance, bought a loaf of eight-grain whole wheat bread and returned home. Walking to the store, I thought about how I was going to get a job for the summer and save my money to buy a car. I heard that Utah Joe's was hiring. I know the waitresses there make good tips and told myself I would apply when I had the chance. Next, I found my way to the mall with Stacey Dok. We shopped and had lunch. I took a shower and ate left-over pizza. At the ball game we watched Karen's sister play softball. They won and we went to Karlie's for shakes. At 8:00 pm Karen and I jetted home to watch the season finale of Daughter Issues. It ended at 10:00 pm and I invited Karen to spend the night. We then took a couple of minutes before going to bed to put out the trash. The trash can was next to the car, so I backed the car out of the garage, put out the trash, and then put the car back in the garage. I guess I probably scraped something when I put the car back. We then started to go to sleep around 3:00 am. That's pretty much it."

Steps

1. Draw a ⌐box around¬ the Occurrence of Significance. Calculate the proportion here:

2. <u>Underline</u> High-Quality Sensory Details.
3. <u>Underline</u> High-Quality Locational Details.
4. Draw a ⌐box¬ around Pivot Words.
5. ~~Mark through~~ Irrelevant Information.
6. Draw a ◯circle◯ around Time Markers.
7. Write ***[GAP]*** where you find Statement Gaps.
8. Draw <angle brackets> around Gap Cover Words.
9. Draw (parentheses) around Uncompleted Action Words.
10. Draw [brackets] around Non-Specific Transit Words.

(Turn page for answers.)

ANSWERS

(Note: See the final summary for explanations of all the answers.)

Occurrence of Significance

> "Let's see ... you left here and I did the dishes and stuff, and other things like that. I walked to Zack's located across the street from the Kingston Park entrance, bought a loaf of eight-grain whole wheat bread and returned home. Walking to the store, I thought about how I was going to get a job for the summer and save my money to buy a car. I heard that Utah Joe's was hiring. I know the waitresses there make good tips and told myself I would apply when I had the chance. Next, I found my way to the mall with Stacey Dok. We shopped and had lunch. I took a shower and ate left-over pizza. At the ball game we watched Karen's sister play softball. They won and we went to Karlie's for shakes. At 8:00 pm Karen and I jetted home to watch the season finale of Daughter Issues. It ended at 10:00 pm and I invited Karen to spend the night. We then took a couple of minutes before going to bed to put out the trash. The trash can was next to the car, so I backed the car out of the garage, put out the trash, and then put the car back in the garage. **I guess I probably scraped something when I put the car back.** We then started to go to sleep around 3:00 am. That's pretty much it."

High-Quality Sensory & Locational Details

"Let's see … you left here and I did the dishes and stuff, and other things like that. I walked to Zack's located across the street from the Kingston Park entrance, bought a loaf of eight-grain whole wheat bread and returned home. Walking to the store, I thought about how I was going to get a job for the summer and save my money to buy a car. I heard that Utah Joe's was hiring. I know the waitresses there make good tips and told myself I would apply when I had the chance. Next, I found my way to the mall with Stacey Dok. We shopped and had lunch. I took a shower and ate left-over pizza. At the ball game we watched Karen's sister play softball. They won and we went to Karlie's for shakes. At 8:00 pm Karen and I jetted home to watch the season finale of Daughter Issues. It ended at 10:00 pm and I invited Karen to spend the night. We then took a couple of minutes before going to bed to put out the trash. The trash can was next to the car, so I backed the car out of the garage, put out the trash, and then put the car back in the garage. I guess I probably scraped something when I put the car back. We then started to go to sleep around 3:00 am. That's pretty much it."

Pivot Words

"Let's see ... you left here and I did the dishes and stuff, and other things like that. I walked to Zack's located across the street from the Kingston Park entrance, bought a loaf of eight-grain whole wheat bread and returned home. Walking to the store, I thought about how I was going to get a job for the summer and save my money to buy a car. I heard that Utah Joe's was hiring. I know the waitresses there make good tips and told myself I would apply when I had the chance. Next, I found my way to the mall with Stacey Dok. We shopped and had lunch. I took a shower and ate left-over pizza. At the ball game we watched Karen's sister play softball. They won and we went to Karlie's for shakes. At 8:00 pm Karen and I jetted home to watch the season finale of Daughter Issues. It ended at 10:00 pm and I invited Karen to spend the night. We then took a couple of minutes before going to bed to put out the trash. The trash can was next to the car, so I backed the car out of the garage, put out the trash, and then put the car back in the garage. I guess I probably scraped something when I put the car back. We then started to go to sleep around 3:00 am. That's pretty much it."

Irrelevant Information

"Let's see ... you left here and I did the dishes and ~~stuff,~~ ~~and other things like that.~~ ~~I walked to Zack's located across the street from the Kingston Park entrance, bought a loaf of eight-grain whole wheat bread and returned home. Walking to the store, I thought about how I was going to get a job for the summer and save my money to buy a car. I heard that Utah Joe's was hiring. I know the waitresses there make good tips and told myself I would apply when I had the chance. Next, I found my way to the mall with Stacey Dok. We shopped and had lunch. I took a shower and ate left-over pizza. At the ball game we watched Karen's sister play softball. They won and we went to Karlie's for shakes. At 8:00 pm Karen and I jetted home to watch the season finale of Daughter Issues.~~ It ended at 10:00 pm and I invited Karen to spend the night. We then took a couple of minutes before going to bed to put out the trash. ~~The trash can was next to the car, so~~ I backed the car out of the garage, put out the trash, and then put the car back in the garage. ~~I guess I probably scraped something when I put the car back.~~ We then started to go to sleep around 3:00 am. That's ~~pretty much it.~~"

Time Markers

"Let's see ... you left here and I did the dishes and stuff, and other things like that. I walked to Zack's located across the street from the Kingston Park entrance, bought a loaf of eight-grain whole wheat bread and returned home. Walking to the store, I thought about how I was going to get a job for the summer and save my money to buy a car. I heard that Utah Joe's was hiring. I know the waitresses there make good tips and told myself I would apply when I had the chance. Next, I found my way to the mall with Stacey Dok. We shopped and had lunch. I took a shower and ate left-over pizza. At the ball game we watched Karen's sister play softball. They won and we went to Karlie's for shakes. At 8:00 pm Karen and I jetted home to watch the season finale of Daughter Issues. It ended at 10:00 pm and I invited Karen to spend the night. We then took a couple of minutes before going to bed to put out the trash. The trash can was next to the car, so I backed the car out of the garage, put out the trash, and then put the car back in the garage. I guess I probably scraped something when I put the car back. We then started to go to sleep around 3:00 am. That's pretty much it."

Statement Gaps

"Let's see ... you left here and I did the dishes and stuff, and other things like that. I walked to Zack's located across the street from the Kingston Park entrance, bought a loaf of eight-grain whole wheat bread and returned home. Walking to the store, I thought about how I was going to get a job for the summer and save my money to buy a car. I heard that Utah Joe's was hiring. I know the waitresses there make good tips and told myself I would apply when I had the chance. Next, I found my way to the mall with Stacey Dok. We shopped and had lunch. *[GAP]* I took a shower and ate left-over pizza. *[GAP]* At the ball game we watched Karen's sister play softball. They won and we went to Karlie's for shakes. At 8:00 pm Karen and I jetted home to watch the season finale of Daughter Issues. It ended at 10:00 pm and I invited Karen to spend the night. We then took a couple of minutes before going to bed to put out the trash. The trash can was next to the car, so I backed the car out of the garage, put out the trash, and then put the car back in the garage. I guess I probably scraped something when I put the car back. We then started to go to sleep around 3:00 am. That's pretty much it."

Gap Cover Words

> "Let's see ... you left here and I did the dishes and stuff, and other things like that. I walked to Zack's located across the street from the Kingston Park entrance, bought a loaf of eight grain whole wheat bread and returned home. Walking to the store, I thought about how I was going to get a job for the summer and save my money to buy a car. I heard that Utah Joe's was hiring. I know the waitresses there make good tips and told myself I would apply when I had the chance. <Next>, I found my way to the mall with Stacey Dok. We shopped and had lunch. *[GAP]* I took a shower and ate left-over pizza. *[GAP]* At the ball game we watched Karen's sister play softball. They won and we went to Karlie's for shakes. At 8:00 pm Karen and I jetted home to watch the season finale of Daughter Issues. It ended at 10:00 pm and I invited Karen to spend the night. We then took a couple of minutes before going to bed to put out the trash. The trash can was next to the car, so I backed the car out of the garage, put out the trash, and then put the car back in the garage. I guess I probably scraped something when I put the car back. We then started to go to sleep around 3:00 am. That's pretty much it."

Uncompleted Action Words

"Let's see ... you left here and I did the dishes and stuff, and other things like that. I walked to Zack's located across the street from the Kingston Park entrance, bought a loaf of eight-grain whole wheat bread and returned home. Walking to the store, I thought about how I was going to get a job for the summer and save my money to buy a car. I heard that Utah Joe's was hiring. I know the waitresses there make good tips and told myself I would apply when I had the chance. <Next>, I found my way to the mall with Stacey Dok. We shopped and had lunch. *[GAP]* I took a shower and ate left-over pizza. *[GAP]* At the ball game we watched Karen's sister play softball. They won and we went to Karlie's for shakes. At 8:00 pm Karen and I jetted home to watch the season finale of Daughter Issues. It ended at 10:00 pm and I invited Karen to spend the night. We then took a couple of minutes before going to bed to put out the trash. The trash can was next to the car, so I backed the car out of the garage, put out the trash, and then put the car back in the garage. I guess I probably scraped something when I put the car back. We then (started) to go to sleep around 3:00 am. That's pretty much it."

Non-Specific Transit Words

"Let's see ... you left here and I did the dishes and stuff, and other things like that. I walked to Zack's located across the street from the Kingston Park entrance, bought a loaf of eight-grain whole wheat bread and returned home. Walking to the store, I thought about how I was going to get a job for the summer and save my money to buy a car. I heard that Utah Joe's was hiring. I know the waitresses there make good tips and told myself I would apply when I had the chance. <Next>, I [found my way] to the mall with Stacey Dok. We shopped and had lunch. [GAP] I took a shower and ate left over pizza. [GAP] At the ball game we watched Karen's sister play softball. They won and we went to Karlie's for shakes. At 8:00 pm Karen and I [jetted] home to watch the season finale of Daughter Issues. It ended at 10:00 pm and I invited Karen to spend the night. We then took a couple of minutes before going to bed to put out the trash. The trash can was next to the car, so I backed the car out of the garage, put out the trash, and then put the car back in the garage. I guess I probably scraped something when I put the car back. We then (started) to go to sleep around 3:00 am. That's pretty much it."

SUMMARY

The **Occurrence of Significance** makes up approximately 4.5 percent of the total statement, which is a small portion and reflects a lack of commitment.

The **High-Quality Sensory and Locational Details** reflect the daughter's commitment, but only to meaningless parts of the statement. She probably did purchase a loaf of eight-grain, whole wheat bread at Zack's and she probably did watch the finale of Daughter Issues. So what? Her parents want to know how their car was damaged. I would prefer to see High-Quality Sensory and Locational Details in or around the Occurrence of Significance.

She uses many **Pivot Words** around the Occurrence of Significance and her parents should consider that she may have used those words to avoid commitment about how the car got damaged.

The daughter's statement has a lot of **Irrelevant Information** and that could be her attempt to create a perception that she is being cooperative and responsive to her parent's inquiry. Additionally, she may have used Irrelevant Information to create the impression that she is someone who completes household-related tasks and is motivated to find a job—all positive character traits that most parents would admire. She may hope that her parents think she isn't the type of person to use a car without permission.

Looking at the **Time Markers** we see that the daughter says she and her friend spent at least five hours between putting out the trash and starting to go to sleep. What happened during those five hours?

The heavy use of **Statement Gaps** and a **Gap Cover Word** could be an attempt by the daughter to avoid committing to what she did before going to the mall, how she got home from the mall, how she got to the softball game, and how she got home from the ball game. What did she do before to going to the mall? How did she get to these places?

The use of an **Uncompleted Action Word** *started* at the end of the statement is interesting. She indicates that she and her friend started the process of going to sleep at around 3:00 am but there is no indication that this action was completed. When did they go to sleep? Did they go to sleep? Could the author be using the word started to mask something else that happened around this time?

Her use of **Non-Specific Transit Words** in her statement could be an attempt to avoid committing to her mode of transportation. Did she use her parents' car? Her use of these Non-Specific Transit Words is especially interesting because we know she is capable of giving specific Transit Words, as she does when she says she walked to the convenience store.

WAS THE CAR DAMAGED IN THE MANNER REPORTED?

This analysis of the daughter's statement shows that she lacks commitment regarding how she traveled to various locations while her parents were away, how their car was damaged, and what she and her friend did for five-plus hours after the car was damaged. Equipped with this analysis, her parents should re-question their daughter with an emphasis on determining her mode of transportation while they were away, determining exactly how the car was damaged, and determining what she did with her friend for five-plus hours after the car was damaged.

SUMMARY CHART

Congratulations! You have finished this book and now the real work begins.

Remember that the knowledge you have acquired can be forgotten if you don't reinforce it through practice. You can never know enough. The science and research that supports this area of linguistics is constantly evolving. Practice what you have learned and read, read, and read some more. Read books, articles, and academic papers about forensic linguistics, statement analysis, text analysis, language, linguistics, and related topics. If you are not sure where to start, I have a number of references listed at the back of this book.

My final note: It is not the intent of this book to give you the ability to determine, with absolute certainty, whether someone is lying or telling the truth. Nobody can do that! The intent of this book is to present specific methodologies for examining statements, to make you more curious about statements, and, in the end, to encourage you to ask more questions about statements. If this book has done that for you then you are well on your way to understanding what people really are saying!

A summary chart of all the methodologies is on the following pages.

"Bit by bit, putting it together... Every little detail plays a part."

— Stephen Sondheim

SUMMARY CHART

METHODOLOGY	SUMMARY	MARK-UP
Occurrence of Significance	Where a statement's author begins to describe being alerted to a significant incident, problem, issue, or concern. It ends when the author indicates that the incident is neutralized or no longer present.	Draw a box around the Occurrence of Significance `Occurrence of Significance`
High-Quality Sensory Details	Specific details using the senses. May reflect commitment to a statement and may indicate veracity in the part of the statement where they are found.	Underline any High-Quality Sensory Details <u>High-Quality Sensory Details</u>
High-Quality Locational Details	Descriptions of specific locations. May show an author's commitment to the part of the statement where they are found. Indicate possible veracity.	Underline any High-Quality Locational Details <u>High-Quality Locational Details</u>
Pivot Words	These words allow a statement author to pivot away from commitment to their statement. Some example words are *probably*, *maybe*, *possibly*, *likely*, and *about*. Pivot Words are also called equivocators, qualifiers, or hedges and they indicate possible deception.	Draw a box around any Pivot Words or phrases Pivot `Word`
Irrelevant Information	Information that has little or no relevance to the question or topic. This tactic can be used to avoid a question, to create a perception, or to explain *why* something happened rather than *what* happened.	Mark through any Irrelevant Information ~~Irrelevant Information~~

SUMMARY CHART

METHODOLOGY	SUMMARY	MARK-UP
Time Markers	References to time, either indirectly or directly. A direct Time Marker is a specific time such as *3:45 pm* or *7:05 in the evening*. An indirect Time Marker is not specific, such as *a couple of hours*, *around six hours ago*, or *close to 3*.	Draw a circle around the Time Markers (Time Marker)
Statement Gaps	Unexpected breaks or interruptions in the flow of a description of activities. Could indicate an author's intent to skip over a portion of their statement.	Write the word GAP in brackets where you find any Statement Gaps Statement **[GAP]** Gap
Gap Cover Words	Words or phrases used to conceal an unexpected break or interruption in the flow of a statement. Words such as *after*, *next*, and *later* are Gap Cover Words.	Draw angle brackets around any Gap Cover Words \<Gap Cover Word\>
Uncompleted-Action Words	These words indicate the start of an action or activity that is not necessarily concluded. Words such as *began* and *proceeded* are Uncompleted-Action Words.	Draw parentheses around any Uncompleted-Action Words **(**Uncompleted-Action**)** Word
Non-Specific Transit Words	Vague and indefinite descriptions of transportation, such as *made my way*, *journeyed*, *traveled to*, and *dipped*.	Draw brackets around any Non-Specific Transit Words Non-Specific **[**Transit**]** Word

REFERENCES

Abbott, H. Porter. (2015). *The Cambridge Introduction to Narrative*. Cambridge University Press.

Adams, S. (2002). *Communication Under Stress: Indicators of veracity and deception in written narratives* [Doctoral dissertation, Virginia Polytechnic Institute and State University].

Adams, S. (2004, April). Statement analysis: Beyond the words. *FBI Law Enforcement Bulletin*, 22-23.

Adams, S. (1996, October). Statement analysis: What do suspects' words really reveal? *FBI Law Enforcement* Bulletin, 12-20.

Adams, S., et al. (October, 2004). Are you telling me the truth: Indicators of veracity in written statements. FBI Law Enforcement Bulletin, 7-12.

Adams, S. & Jarvis, J. (2006). Indicators of veracity and deception: An analysis of written statements made to police. *International Journal of Speech, Language and the Law*, *13*(1), 1-22.

Akmajian, A., et al. (2001). *Linguistics: An introduction to language and communication*. The MIT Press.

Arciuli, J., et al. (2010). Um, I can tell you're lying: Linguistic markers of deception versus truth-telling in speech. *Applied Psycholinguistics*, *31*, 397-411.

Austin, J. L. (1975). *How to Do Things with Words*. Harvard University Press.

Bhattacharjee, Y. (2017, July). Why we lie: The science behind our deceptive ways. *National Geographic*.

Bowers, J., et al. (1977, Spring). Exploiting pragmatic rules: Devious messages. *Human Communication Research*, *3*(1), 235-242.

Buller, D.B., and Burgoon, J.K. (1996). Interpersonal deception theory. *Communication Theory*, 6, 203-242.

Cannon, W.B. (1915). *Bodily changes in pain, hunger, fear and rage: An account of recent researches into the function of emotional excitement*. Forgotten Books, 2018.

Coulthard, M. & Johnson, A. (2007). *An introduction to forensic linguistics: Language in evidence*. Routledge.

Cruse, A. (2009). *Meaning in language: An introduction to semantics and pragmatics*. Oxford University Press.

de Becker, G. (2000). *The gift of fear*. Bloomsbury Publishing.

DePaulo, B. (2019). *The psychology of lying and detecting lies*. Create Space Independent Publishing Platform.

DePaulo, B., et al. (2003). Cues to deception. *Psychological Bulletin*, *129*(1), 74-118.

Dulaney, E. (1982, Fall). Changes in language behavior as a function of veracity. *Human Communication Research*, *9*(1), 73-82.

Ekman, P. (2009). *Telling lies: Clues to deceit in the marketplace, politics, and marriage*. W. W. Norton and Company.

Fisher, R. P. & Geiselman, E. R. (1992). *Memory-enhancement techniques for investigative interviewing: The cognitive interview.* Charles C Thomas Publisher.

Green, M. (2016, January 17). How the brain reacts to scrambled stories: Research shows that people tend to prefer linear narratives, but can also be engaged by just the right amount of disruption. *The Atlantic.* https://www.theatlantic.com/health/archive/2016/01/linear-storytelling-psychology/431529/

Grice, P. (1991). *Studies in the way of words.* Harvard University Press.

Hess, J. E. (2010). *Interviewing & interrogation for law enforcement.* Routledge.

Horowitz, S. W., et al. (1997). Reliability of criteria-based content analysis of child witness statements. *Legal and Criminological Psychology, 2,* 11-22.

Houston, P., Floyd, M., Carnicero, S. & Tennant, D. (2012). *Spy the lie.* St. Martin's Griffin.

Johnson, M. K. & Raye, C.L. (1981). Reality monitoring. *Psychological Review, 88*(1), 67-85.

Johnson, M. K., et al. (1988). Phenomenal characteristics of memories for perceived and imagined autobiographical events. *Journal of Experimental Psychology: General, 117*(4), 371-376.

Klopf, G. & Tooke, A. (2000, April). Statement analysis field examination technique: A useful investigative tool. *FBI Law Enforcement Bulletin,* 6-4.

Knapp, Mark L., et al. (1974). An exploration of deception as a communication construct. *Human Communication Research, 1,* 15-29.

Knapp, M. L. & Comadena, M.E. (1979). Telling it like it isn't: A review of theory and research on deceptive communications. *Human Communication Research, 5*(3), 270-285.

Knapp, M. L., et al. (2016). *Lying and deception in human interaction.* Kendall Hunt.

Lamb, M. E. & Sternberg, K. J., (1997). Criterion-based content analysis: A field validation study. *Child Abuse & Neglect, 21*(3), 255-264.

Levinson, S. C. (2010). *Pragmatics.* Routledge.

Martinie, M., et al. (2010). Cognitive dissonance induced by writing counter-attitudinal essay facilitates performance on simple tasks but not on complex tasks that involve working memory. *Journal of Experimental Social Psychology, 46,* 587-594.

Milne, R. & Bull, R. (2008). *Investigative interviewing: Psychology and practice.* John Wiley & Sons.

McCornack, S., et al. (March, 1996). Speaking of information manipulation: A critical rejoinder. *Communication Monographs, 63,* 83-92.

McGlone, M. S. & Knapp, M. L. (2010). *The interplay of truth and deception: New agendas in communication.* Routledge.

McLeod, S. (2023, June 16) Long-term Memory in Psychology: Types, capacity, and duration. *Simply Psychology.* simplypsychology.org/long-term-memory.html.

McWhorter, J. (2016, November). The evolution of "like". *The Atlantic.*

Miller, B. (2010). *Wilson & Sperber's Relevance Theory: Seminar paper.* Druck und Bindung Books on Demand.

Miller, G. R. & Stiff, J. B. (1993). *Deceptive communication.* Sage Publications.

Morgan, C. A., et al. (2011). Efficacy of forensic statement analysis in distinguishing truthful from deceptive eyewitness accounts of highly stressful events. *Journal of Forensic Sciences, 56*(5), 1227-1234.

Newman, M. L., et al. (2003, May). Lying words: Predicting deception from linguistic styles. *Personality and Social Psychology Bulletin, 29*(5), 665-675.

Pagel, M. (2017) Q and A: What is human language, when did it evolve, and why should we care? *BMC Biology,* 15 (64), 1-6.

Pei, M. (1969). *Glossary of Linguistic Terminology.* Columbia University Press.

Pennebaker, J. (2011). *The secret life of pronouns.* Bloomsbury Press.

Porter, S. & Brinke, L. (2010). The truth about lies: What works in detecting high-stakes deception? *Legal and Criminological Psychology, 15,* 57-75.

Porter, S. and Yuille, J. C. (1995). Credibility assessment of criminal suspects through statement analysis. *Psychology, Crime & Law, 1,* 319-331.

Rabon, D. (1994). *Investigative discourse analysis.* Carolina Academic Press.

Rabon, D. (2012). *Investigative discourse analysis: Statements, letters, and transcripts.* Carolina Academic Press.

Raskin, D. & Esplin, P. (1991). Statement validity and assessment: Interview procedures and content analysis of children's statement of sexual abuse. *Behavioral Assessment, 13,* 265-291.

Rudacille, W.C. (1994). *Identifying lies in disguise.* Kendall Hunt Publishing.

Rudacille, W. C. (1994). *Verbal based detection of deception, interviewing & interrogation.* IDLies Publishing.

Riessman, C. K. (1993). *Narrative analysis.* SAGE Publications.

Sandoval, V. A. (2008, January). Interview clues: Words that leave an investigative trail. *FBI Law Enforcement Bulletin,* 2-8.

Sandoval, V. A. (2003, October). Strategies to avoid interview contamination. *FBI Law Enforcement Bulletin,* 1-12.

Schaefer, J. (2011, June). Blurred truth Is still the truth. *Psychology Today.*

Schaefer, J. (2019). *Psychological narrative analysis: A professional method to detect deception in written and oral communications.* Charles C. Thomas Publisher.

Schaefer, J. (2011, June). Reading people by the words they speak: Word clues present a noninvasive technique to effectively read people. *Psychology Today.*

Schaefer, J. R. (2008). Text bridges and the micro-action interview. *FBI Law Enforcement Bulletin,* 20-24.

Schiffrin, D. (1990). *Discourse markers: Studies in interactional sociolinguistics.* Cambridge University Press.

Shepherd, E. & Griffiths, A. (2001). *Investigative interviewing.* Oxford University Press.

Smith, D. (2004). *Why we lie: Evolutionary roots of deception and the unconscious mind.* St. Martin's Press.

Stein, N., et al. (1997). *Memory for everyday and emotional events.* Lawrence Erlbaum Associates, Publishers.

Strauss, S. & Feiz, P. (2014). *Discourse analysis: Putting our worlds into words.* Routledge.

Turvey, B. E., et al. (2018). *False allegations: Investigative and forensic issues in fraudulent reports of crime.* Academic Press.

Undeutsch, Udo. (1989). The development of statement reality analysis. *Nato Science, 47,* 101-119.

Varnell, S. (2013). *Statement analysis: An ISS Course Workbook.* SCV Publishing.

Vrij, A., et al. (2000). The effect of informing liars about Criteria-Based Content Analysis on their ability to deceive CBCA raters. Legal and Criminological Psychology, *5,* 57-70.

Vrij, A. (2005, March). Criteria-based content analysis: A qualitative review of the first 37 studies. *Psychology, Public Policy and Law. 11*(1), 3-41.

Vrij, A. (2008). *Detecting lies and deceit: Pitfalls and opportunities.* John Wiley and Sons Publishing.

Weintraub, W. (1993). *Verbal behavior in everyday life.* Springer Publishing.

Wells, R. C. (2008, January). The art of investigative interviewing: Countering the lie of omission. *FBI Law Enforcement Bulletin,* 2-11.

White, C. H. (2008). *Engaging theories in interpersonal communication: Multiple perspectives.* Sage Publications. 2008.

Zaparniuk, J., et al. (1995). Assessing the credibility of true and false statements. *International Journal of Law and Psychiatry, 18*(3), 343-352.

Zimmerman, L. (2016, March). Deception detection. *American Psychological Association, 47*(3), 46.

NOTES

NOTES

NOTES

NOTES

ABOUT THE AUTHOR

Stanley B. Burke worked in law enforcement for more than 25 years, first as a police officer and investigator for the Maryland-National Capital Park Police and then as a special agent, instructor, and supervisor for the FBI. As an FBI field agent Burke worked in the Phoenix, Dallas, and Albuquerque Divisions where he investigated homicides, robberies, kidnappings, sexual assaults, murder-for-hire plots, and organized crime.

He was then assigned to the FBI Academy in Quantico, Virginia, where he taught Interviewing and Interrogation Through Statement Analysis to both undergraduate and graduate students. Following that, he was appointed unit chief for the FBI's Law Enforcement Communication Resources Unit, where he worked with the FBI's Behavioral Sciences Unit and founded the FBI's Joint Communication Exploitation Research Team. This team analyzed statements submitted by law enforcement agencies worldwide and became an invaluable investigative resource. In 2010 FBI Director Robert Mueller awarded Burke the prestigious FBI Director's Award for these efforts.

After retiring from the FBI in 2011, he earned certification as a forensic interviewer and currently provides interviewing, interrogation, and investigative statement analysis services and instruction to law enforcement, intelligence, military, and security clients throughout the world. He has assisted in the successful resolution of many high-profile cases including one of the longest cold-case homicide prosecutions in the history of the United States.

He has lectured widely in academic settings, made multiple television appearances, consulted on podcasts, and been published in many law enforcement-related magazines and journals.

Comments or interested in learning more?
Go to www.precisionintelligenceconsulting.com

ACKNOWLEDGEMENTS

Thanks to my wife Mary Coffman-Burke for taking the time and energy to turn this idea into reality. Thanks to Benjamin Burke and Rebekah Burke for always listening, supporting, and contributing to your old man's ideas. Thanks to Jeff Green, Mike Dougherty, Rudy Flores, Mike Atchison, and my nephew Jimmy Murray for your feedback, encouragement, and friendship. I owe you one!

www.ingramcontent.com/pod-product-compliance
Lightning Source LLC
Chambersburg PA
CBHW040004040426
42337CB00033B/5216